D. H. Lawrence and Frieda

First published in 2008 by André Deutsch
An imprint of the Carlton Publishing Group
20 Mortimer Street
London
W1T 3JW

1 3 5 7 9 10 8 6 4 2

A CIP catalogue record for this book is available from
the British Library.

ISBN 978 0 233 00232 3

Printed in the UK

D. H. Lawrence and Frieda

A portrait of love and loyalty

Michael Squires

André Deutsch

To Lynn

"To me, loyalty is far before love."

D. H. Lawrence to Thomas Seltzer, 4 January 1923

Picture Credits

Acknowledgements

My wife, Lynn K. Talbot, deserves thanks far beyond those usually owed to a spouse. She spent many years collecting, dating and annotating more than two thousand of Frieda Lawrence's letters. I have benefited from her resourceful scholarship, her discovery of unpublished materials, her answers to hundreds of questions, her help with translations and her thoughtful readings of my manuscript. I dedicate this book to her.

As he has done for 35 years, Keith Cushman read my text with his customary wisdom, intelligence and knowledge of the Lawrences. On every page he offered incisive suggestions, saw angles I had missed and challenged my conclusions. I thank him for his exceptional generosity.

Others who read the manuscript also suggested improvements. With eyes on the speed and clarity of the narrative, my son Andrew Squires offered valuable comments, as did Michael Diaz, my student at Virginia Tech, who read the manuscript with keen understanding.

At Pollinger Limited I am grateful to Tim Bates for suggesting the content and shape of the book and for making available unpublished documents. At André Deutsch I wish to thank Penny Phillips and Penny Craig for their fine professional assistance.

For many other contributions I thank James N. O'Neill, Alexander W. Scott, Paul and Peg Sorrentino, Cameron Squires, Kelly M. Squires, Elmer Turman and Louise E. Wright. At Virginia Tech, Connie Stovall helped me explore the history of Mexico in the 1920s. Stefania Michelluci

ACKNOWLEDGEMENTS

shared with me her interview with Stefano Ravagli. For checking my translations, I thank Martina E. Retter, Giuliana Chapman and Nick Ceramella. John Worthen and Cornelia Rumpf-Worthen kindly let me use their superb translations of Frieda Lawrence's *sütterlin* letters held at the University of Texas at Austin. In San Cristobal, New Mexico, Jenny Vincent, drawing on her astonishing memory, identified obscure places and people the Lawrences had known; my gratitude to her is immense.

Libraries that granted permission to quote from unpublished materials include Harry Ransom Humanities Research Center, University of Texas at Austin; Manuscripts and Special Collections, University of Nottingham; Fray Angélico Chávez History Library, Santa Fe, New Mexico; Beinecke Rare Book and Manuscript Library, Yale University; McCormick Library of Special Collections, Northwestern University; Special Collections Research Center, Southern Illinois University at Carbondale; Center for Southwest Research, University of New Mexico; James S. Copley Library; and Special Collections, Stanford University. Individuals who granted permission to quote from unpublished materials include Barbara Horgan, Catherine Stoye, and Rosalind Wells.

Finally, for permission to use unpublished materials of the Lawrences, I owe special thanks to Lesley Pollinger of Pollinger Limited and to the Estate of Frieda Lawrence Ravagli.

Blacksburg, Virginia
February 2008

Contents

Selected Works by D. H. Lawrence

Except for drafts of novels, I cite date of first publication.

>‑⦿‑○‑⦿‑‑◄

1926	*The First Lady Chatterley* (novel, first published 1944)
1927	*The Second Lady Chatterley* (novel, first published 1972)
1927	*Mornings in Mexico* (travel)
1928	*Lady Chatterley's Lover* (novel, abridged edition published 1932)
1928	*The Woman Who Rode Away and Other Stories*
1928	*The Collected Poems of D. H. Lawrence*
1929	*The Paintings of D. H. Lawrence*
1931	*Apocalypse* (philosophy)
1932	*Sketches of Etruscan Places* (travel)
1932	*The Letters of D. H. Lawrence*
1933	*The Plays of D. H. Lawrence*
1979–2000	*The Letters of D. H. Lawrence*, 8 volumes (complete letters)
1984	*Mr Noon* (autobiographical fiction)

Preface

For D. H. Lawrence, one of the great writers of the 20th century, marriage was the central relationship that stimulated and enriched him. His wife Frieda von Richthofen felt the same. Examining the struggles that both ennobled and diminished them, this book offers a portrait of affectionate commitment shaded with betrayal. But most important, it offers a portrait of love and loyalty and the challenges these ideals posed to a sensitive writer and his wilful wife.

The book aims to be candid, spirited, fresh and succinct. It digests, at times quotes, many new materials. My wife and I spent a dozen years collecting two thousand of Frieda's letters for a complete edition. More than one thousand are unpublished. I often draw on them to make the Lawrences stand bolder and bigger than before.

Lawrence and Frieda were an unconventional couple. They lived with such intensity that their bond, though it fractured, grew remarkably strong. Just a few years ago, they were the subject of unfriendly anecdotes – as figures carping at each other in front of dismayed onlookers. Luckily, new materials sometimes correct old impressions, and stabilize the truth with facts. For instance,

- The new letters confirm Lawrence's integrity as man and writer. What Frieda said after he died – that he was "a great and plucky soul" – she could have said when they met. An adventurer in human emotion, he toppled walls and, in his fiction, opened gates in all the places marked "Do Not Enter".

- The new letters gauge the meaning of Frieda's father's affair with a woman named Selma, who bore him a son in 1897, then continued to demand money – "a thousand Marks", Frieda once heard. For her father to remain in a loveless marriage served as a warning. Frieda saw all too plainly "how this living together, empty inside, is *deadly* for human beings". Monogamy had its perils.

- The new letters reveal the vibrant, stimulating companion Frieda was – not the quarrelsome, tempestuous person she was often thought to be, but a warm, lively, opinionated conversationalist who in later years cultivated strong friendships.

- Together with unpublished materials at the Chávez Library in New Mexico, the new letters more precisely fix Lawrence's income, which eventually grew large enough to permit expensive living, and they detail Frieda's income after his death and the many possibilities it allowed.

- The new letters also explore Frieda's energetic efforts to rescue Lawrence's posthumous reputation, which collapsed until about 1950. Her letters after 1930 capture her hard at work – locating his letters, recovering his ashes from France, selling his handwritten manuscripts, adapting his novel *The Plumed Serpent* for Hollywood, pressing for dramatizations of *Lady Chatterley's Lover*, his most famous novel, and in 1954 urging the Grove Press in New York to reprint the original (more explicit) text of *Lady Chatterley*. Frieda's freewheeling negotiations, aided by Aldous Huxley and other friends, were both adept and offbeat.

Such materials freshly shape this new portrait. It is a surprise that the chafing irritation the Lawrences tolerated – between themselves, and with those around them – did not break their bond. But it did not. Because Lawrence was contentious, and Frieda equally so, their friction sometimes led to unrest. Yet the stirrings of wonder, which each felt in and from the other, bound them powerfully. It is easy to say that Lawrence and Frieda were complements, or that their stars created a balanced equilibrium, but that's a partial view – as when one covers an eye and loses the perception of depth. The truth is more interesting.

In truth, Lawrence and Frieda were unwavering in their identities; they knew themselves so well, had been so fully tested by struggle and tragedy, that they could demand a strong connection. In 1912 Lawrence marvelled, "I've got a mate and I'll fight tooth and claw to keep her". Four years later he allowed that, despite their fights, "Frieda and I become more and more truly married" – and he himself "more and more unified". Yet, being so stringently alive, they refused to settle for love at the price of obligation or pity or mere infatuation. When they met, both had strong loyalties – Lawrence to his mother (by then, dead), Frieda to her children. These loyalties had to be broken – and the breaking cost them both dearly. "Lawrence and I know we have done the right thing," Frieda wrote in 1912, "though there was a lot of wrong in it."

From Frieda's admission derives a second notion. Out of the breakage of past loyalties developed not the hand-in-glove "fit" typical of idealized marriages. Something else developed: a sharp crosscut of temperaments that formed layers of mutual antagonism, affection, stimulation and peace. The Lawrences' bond provided security *as well as* anxiety; they negotiated their differences, but, as sparring partners, embraced at the end of every match. As in any relationship, the charm and delight they found in each other required frequent adjustment. After World War I – and the drastic toll it took – they finally accepted their status as outcasts and were for ever altered: they were required to live more and more inside each other, especially when they visited the exotic cultures of Ceylon, Australia, Mexico, and the Taos Indians of the United States. Such intense living created ambivalence – an uneasy cluster of power, infidelity

PREFACE

and disappointment that often tested their loyalty *and* their love. That they sometimes failed the test makes their story all the more appealing.

After Lawrence's death, Frieda regained the fullness and force of what he had given her – freedom of thought, a sustaining belief in her capacity to love, and a new life in Taos, New Mexico, stripped to essentials. In Taos (she wrote in 1934), had Lawrence still been alive, "I would have everything". Before her death she recognized that "A woman can only have *one* husband in a lifetime!" As the years passed, loyalty and love narrowed to devotion, as Frieda zealously promoted Lawrence's work in print and film. No matter that she was often unsuccessful. She complained to agents, negotiated with film moguls, resisted arrogant university deans, and prodded reluctant editors – all to secure Lawrence's legacy as man and artist.

Indeed, the Lawrences travelled their own road – from inflicting "wrong" on others, to embracing their destiny as "lifetime" mates. As the road unwinds through their lives, it may offer sharp turns and dead-ends, but it shows a lasting human commitment that even flagrant lapses could not prise apart.

This new portrait gives readers the Lawrences' most essential qualities – their joy in each other, and the shadows its frustration cast. An unpublished letter, full of delighted irony, captures the essence of their bond. In 1914 Frieda wrote to her brother-in-law, Edgar Jaffe, "You know us – turtle-doves as always, who only coo softly, especially the male dove!" But the cooing was seldom soft, and the male dove could sometimes shout. Edgar Jaffe would have understood that it was Frieda who stirred Lawrence to fresh perception, who made him confront the truths about respect, attraction and fidelity which he might not have found on his own. In this biography, her forceful character and its influence appear more clearly than before, and the love and loyalty that bound the Lawrences can be given its full expression.

➤◆➤◦◄◆◄

Chapter 1
Two Lonely People

They met in 1912. Lawrence was charming but unsophisticated – a British lad with a good education, no money and a provincial outlook. Standing five feet nine inches, he had light hair, a narrow chest and quick movements. Near London, he spent long days teaching a class of ten-year-old boys and, in the evenings, writing poems and stories; in 1911 he had distinguished himself by publishing a novel, *The White Peacock*. Frieda was already a mature woman. She had a statuesque frame, green eyes and an ebullient temperament – but was bored by her life with a Nottingham professor named Ernest Weekley. Often idle, she read books, played the piano and took long walks. A nanny cared for her three children – daughters aged seven and nine, and a son, eleven – who loved their mother's sense of fun.

Both Lawrence and Frieda were lonely. The force that brought them together was a deep need for completion, though anyone who met them would have thought them unsuited for more than friendship. In those days class barriers functioned as gates, keeping people off one another's turf. Lawrence was working class, often proud of it – yet shared his mother's snobbery. Though not rich, Frieda's father, a German baron named Friedrich von Richthofen, had given her the fine assurance of an aristocrat. Casting aside their class differences, Lawrence and Frieda met several times in the spring – her husband had introduced them – and made excursions into the Midlands countryside. Once, when

Lawrence made Frieda's young daughters some paper boats and floated them down a stream, she gazed at him and, in a flash of revelation, knew she had fallen in love. In some curious way he completed her. She couldn't say why – she wasn't analytical. But in her heart she knew. His vitality erased her loneliness; his clever understanding curbed her rashness; and his frail physique invited her protection.

For his part, Lawrence was powerfully attracted to this intelligent woman, aged 32. Her strong body, straight nose and bold, throaty laughter intrigued him. To his friend and mentor, Edward Garnett, he wrote in April, "[S]he's splendid, she is really [...] perfectly unconventional, but really good – in the best sense. I'll bet you've never met anybody like her, by a long chalk. [...] Oh but she is the woman of a lifetime." Still cautious, Lawrence told no one in his family about Frieda. Both his sisters, to whom he was close, would have disapproved. Frieda was married!

Lydia, Lawrence's beloved mother, had died 16 months earlier in Eastwood, the English village where she had lived since 1875 with a husband she had come to despise. The wound her death had inflicted on her favourite son hadn't healed. By 1912 Lawrence, having been so ill that he had given up his job as a schoolmaster, had grown restless and peevish. He too was bored – even with his pretty fiancée Louisa Burrows, also a teacher. Dead set on change, he wanted to break with England and its narrow piety. So did Frieda. They had both become "perfectly unconventional".

Smitten, Frieda soon proposed a plan – to go with Lawrence to the (then German) city of Metz (where she had been brought up), for the jubilee of her father's 50th year in state service, and discover the full scale of their attraction. In her autobiography she wrote, "We [...] crossed the grey channel sitting on some ropes, full of hope and agony. There was nothing but the grey sea, and the dark sky, and the throbbing of the ship, and ourselves." Dark skies, children left behind, families unaware – the signs were ominous.

>–•–>–•–○–•–<–•–<

Clinging to "ourselves" might be especially hard when their contrary qualities emerged. Indeed, Frieda's temerity left space for a gushing tenderness; Lawrence's timidity left space for a scruffy ferocity. Though Frieda may have been the stronger, both embodied many overlapping qualities of character.

In Metz, where the von Richthofen house was full of guests, Lawrence and Frieda stayed at the Hotel Deutscher Hof, secretly meeting her two sisters, the intellectual Else and the chic Johanna. But when Frieda's parents discovered she had entangled herself with a penniless author, they scolded their wayward daughter and insisted she return to her children and her fine home in Nottingham. Her mother Anna von Richthofen had already made the same bargain. Without much complaint, she had endured a long and loveless marriage.

Though Lawrence won over both Else and Johanna, he minded all the upset and domestic strife. He left Metz to visit his cousin, Hannah, in Waldbröl, Germany, and from there wrote Frieda a moving letter: "Dear God, I am marrying you, now, don't you see. It's a far greater thing than ever I knew. [...] I shall love you all my life. That also is a new idea to me. [...] Because, I'm not coming to you now for rest, but to start living. It's a marriage, not a meeting. What an inevitable thing it seems. [...] I know we are right." He spoke from the heart, with confidence and conviction. Born again through Frieda, he felt an intense sense of relief. His confession, rare in any relationship, was an anchor in the tumult. Though often tested, his deep loyalty to Frieda rarely wavered. When the couple finally met in May, near Munich, their passion flowered. Wandering up the Isar Valley, they spent a week in idyllic bliss – hiking the hills, sitting beside lakes, gathering golden bachelor's buttons – then borrowed a châlet in the village of Icking. Detesting the stink of scandal, Lawrence determined he would always live abroad. Above all, he valued the freedom to be himself.

><><>•O•<><><

CHAPTER 1

For Frieda the break was harder. Torn between her growing love for Lawrence and her loyalty to her three children, she went wild with grief. As Lawrence explained to Garnett in July, "She lies on the floor in misery – and then is fearfully angry with me because I won't say 'stay for my sake'. I say 'decide what you want most, to live with me and share my rotten chances, or go back to security, and your children – decide for *yourself* – Choose for yourself.' [...] The letters today [from England] have nearly sent us both crazy. I didn't know life was so hard."

From England, letters from her husband Ernest and others, full of fury, were lashes from those who had been Frieda's gaolers. Her choice was cruel. Ultimately, she ignored the advice pressed on her. Her husband's admonitions to recall her birth and to ditch the coalminer's son ("that filthy hound") made her desperate for Lawrence's love and assurance. Yet sometimes his own commitment appeared tentative or ambiguous. Locked in opposition, they fought bravely: "we nearly murder each other", Lawrence laughed. To find grounds for peace, they hurled themselves into the work of shaping together the final draft of Lawrence's daring new novel, published a year later as *Sons and Lovers*. It lyrically describes a young man's initiation into the mysteries of work and sex, but it also records, like a series of photographs, the life of working-class England.

Lawrence too proposed a plan – to find a place of their own, away from the narrowness of Germany or England. With barely any money, he and Frieda would trek over the Alps, through Austria, and into Italy. Going south mostly on foot, they would steal some bliss out of their misery. On 5 August they shouldered their packs and left the châlet in Icking; walked (often in rain) to Mayrhofen in Austria; fixed their meals by the cold streams; slept in hayhuts when they got lost in the mountains; then rested at a farmhouse. "Frieda and I," Lawrence wrote, "have struggled through some bad times into a wonderful naked intimacy, all kindled

>⊷⊶•O•⊷⊶◄

8

with warmth, that I know at last is love." Their new bond – and its implied loyalty – would soon be tested.

Joining them in Mayrhofen were Edward Garnett's son Bunny, aged 20, and his comrade, Harold Hobson, aged 21. One day while Bunny and Lawrence hunted alpine flowers on the mountain slopes, Frieda responded to Harold's strong masculine appeal. Her appetite was great. She had been hounded by monogamy far too long to miss this opportunity. Lawrence must understand her intolerance of shackles. Her need for freedom was like his, only expressed differently. He wanted a new morality, she wanted amorality.

Not until Bunny and Harold had departed did Frieda tell Lawrence. Although he blamed Harold, Lawrence nobly accepted her avowed aversion to monogamy. He also knew that five years earlier, near Munich, Frieda had yielded to Otto Gross, the drug-addicted poet of Freudian psychoanalysis. Mesmerized by his intellect and strange passion, she preserved his many letters, in which he called her magnificent and magisterial, and himself "inseparably yours". One special letter helped her to see herself as a woman pristine and unpolluted. Gross wrote, "I know it through you, the only human being who already, today, has remained free from the code of chastity, from Christianity, from democracy – remained free through her own strength ... [from] the curse and the dirt of two gloomy millennia." Such delicious warbling gave Frieda a new sense of her potential as a woman with a deep capacity for love. Monogamy might, she thought, simply express fear of openness.

Lawrence, however, came out of an evangelical tradition that castigated adulterers. Though he minded Frieda's disloyalty (he prized his own loyalty so much), he also acknowledged her principled differences and respected them. He knew that she had spent summers soaking up the cultural ferment in Munich, where ideas – revolutionary ideas – blew like pollen from the tree of anarchy. In 1907 the old German order of patriarchy and oppression was breaking up. Like

Frieda, Lawrence also believed in revolutionary ideas. What he wrote in 1911 he preached to Frieda (who needed little persuading): "My great religion is a belief in the blood, the flesh, as being wiser than the intellect. We can go wrong in our minds. But what our blood feels and believes and says, is always true. [...] I conceive a man's body as a kind of flame [...] and the intellect is just the light that is shed onto the things around." He boldly repositioned mind under body.

New ideas festered everywhere. The atom had been split in 1910, X-rays discovered, relativity established as a theory. Having broken from their families – and their pasts – Lawrence and Frieda were ready to embrace the future. They climbed over the snowy mountains and descended into Italy. Loving its beauty and openness, they made their way to Lake Garda, and on to the village of Gargnano, where, speaking no Italian, they found the lakeside Villa Igéa, with four huge rooms and a sunny garden, backed by lemon trees and vineyards. On 18 September they moved in. At last Lawrence had a quiet place to write. Frieda wrote to her mother:

> We have found something so splendid! [...] A flat in a villa with garden and lake, *everything* furnished beautifully and bright. I am happy. [...] I feel sorry for people who slave their lives away when, here, one can live so well for so little money. [...] I can go swimming in the lake straight from the house, and it is quite indescribably beautiful!

Frieda's spontaneous delight in the landscape helped her forget the silent pleas of her children, who were now living in London with their father's parents (see Illustration 3) and sister Maude. They couldn't comprehend why their mother had left them. Frieda's son, Montague, now twelve, had barely eaten since she had left Nottingham in May. How could she protect the children while living with Lawrence and recovering her dream of freedom? How long could she stand to be without them?

Chapter 2
Eastwood and Metz

>──┤─◆>─○─<◆─├─<

Living in Italy gave the Lawrences stimulation and wonder, yet also peace. While Frieda worried about how to see her three children, either in Italy or in England, Lawrence focused on *Sons and Lovers* and wrote brilliant travel sketches, published as *Twilight in Italy*. Fascinated by his creative power, Frieda watched his words "pour out of his hand onto the paper, unconsciously [...] as flowers bloom". Sometimes she would help him imagine what his characters in *Sons and Lovers* felt – and then argue for their beliefs. The novel became a joint venture, full of surprises and disagreements. Frieda had read enough George Eliot to understand social realism; her judgement was sure; and she fearlessly expressed her opinion. In November, Lawrence submitted the manuscript to Duckworth in London, for spring publication. In every way he had made his novel "like life"; and Frieda judged him "so plucky and honest in his work", and his writing so vivid, that "it knocks you down". Duckworth generously advanced Lawrence £100 for the novel – it was like a year's salary. He and Frieda were thrilled. They had love, freedom and months of unfettered time. The fact that they knew no one in Gargnano encouraged them to spend hours talking about their pasts. His was entirely different from hers.

From the outset David Herbert Lawrence, nicknamed Bert, was frail. Born on 11 September 1885, in the red-brick Midlands village of Eastwood, the fourth of five

>──┤─◆>─○─<◆─├─<

children and the youngest son, Lawrence joined a bickering, impoverished family (see Illustration 1). Living in a cramped four-room row house, not far from the Brinsley mine where his father Arthur Lawrence hewed coal, he loved indoor games like charades, adventure books like *Treasure Island*, and pastimes like landscape painting. Bright and spirited, he avoided the village's rough-and-tumble boys and their combat sports. Yet he wasn't weak. He drew strength from the miners' ingrained scepticism and from his religion. With his mother Lydia and sisters, Emily and Ada, he attended the Congregational Chapel on Nottingham Road, learning to cultivate a bond between himself and God which allowed powerful "unknown" forces to pulse through him. Later his religious rapture sometimes turned to satire. He entertained Frieda by acting out the drama of a revival meeting – the sentimental hymns, the preacher's desperate laments for lost souls, the "saved" wretches creeping forward into the golden light of salvation. "Lawrence," Frieda wrote, "made me shake with laughter."

In his early years he preferred his mother's responsible sobriety and honesty to his father's rough ways, which included binges of drinking. Lydia valued her personal convictions and passed to Bert her fierce ambition – and her iron determination that the dark mines would never see his handsome face. Instead, at the age of twelve, Lawrence won a scholarship to Nottingham High School, eight miles from Eastwood, and – ironically – suffered rigours almost equal to those in the mines. Each morning he left home at 7 o'clock, caught the train to Nottingham, mustered full energy all day, then didn't arrive home till 7 in the evening. Money was scarce. "Every little thing we needed extra," he told a friend, "meant saving and scraping for, and not having enough to eat." Despite these privations, he worked hard, was able and imaginative, and behaved well. But few miners' sons had ever attended the school. Socially he mingled with the middle classes but never joined them. Above them in intellect, below them in status, he was an outsider.

Having no money for college, Lawrence agreed to work as an errand boy in a Nottingham factory called Haywoods. By December, listless and pale, he was ill with pneumonia and (with penicillin decades from discovery) stayed in bed for months. Since an untreated infection had recently killed Lawrence's ambitious older brother, Ernest, his mother's anguish at Bert's slide into illness was acute. She hovered closely, her love intensifying into adoration. Their bond tightened into a grip, astounding but unhealthy. Once mended, Lawrence responded to his mother's urging and in October 1902 agreed to train as an apprentice teacher at the British School in Eastwood. He was 17 and, to save money, lived at home. The apprenticeship lasted four years. During this time he matured into a fair-haired, fine-featured, thin-shouldered man – sensitive, creative and disciplined, even as he chafed against the restrictions imposed on him. George Holderness, his supervisor, described him as "hard-working and painstaking, energetic and bright in his manner", but also considerate and kind.

Earlier, in 1901, he had met at church a fellow teacher's apprentice named Jessie Chambers. Living on a farm two miles from Eastwood, she offered him a feast of fresh experience – fragrant meadows, grazing cows and horses, barn swings, a garden with new potatoes, country walks across open fields, and parents – Edmund and Ann – who were affable and polite. A new life took root in him there. He trusted Jessie, lent her books, and drew close to her – until, that is, his mother's disapproval forced him to subdue his passion. No matter. Jessie's terror of sex made her too inhibited for a young man who wanted to buck Victorian prudery. Lawrence was soon writing stories like "The White Stocking", in which a married woman, Elsie Whiston, finds herself dangerously drawn to a man with elegance, class and power. As they dance,

> His fingers seemed to search into her flesh [...] she felt she would give way utterly, and sink molten: the fusion point was coming when she would fuse down into perfect unconsciousness at his feet and knees. But [...] he seemed to sustain all her body with his limbs, his body; and his warmth seemed to come closer into her, nearer, till it would fuse right through her, and she would be as liquid to him, as an intoxication only. It was exquisite.

This kind of writing – sensuous and tactile – gave voice to the erotic electricity that contemporary writers had shunned. Lawrence was marking territory alien to Jessie. It would be his most fertile ground.

Having worked his way up to the level of uncertified assistant teacher, Lawrence, in order to advance, needed a teaching certificate. This he earned at Nottingham University College from 1906 to 1908. Although he dutifully completed his assignments, he didn't flourish. He was bored. Jessie remembered that his interest "centred on his writing and not on his studies". Except for his lessons in botany, he felt he had mostly wasted his time. Teacher "prep" had not challenged him. Yet he still needed to earn an income.

Finally, a successful job interview led him to teach at Davidson Road School, in the outer London suburb of Croydon. The salary was a modest £95 a year, which paid for lodging with a neighbourhood family, weekend entertainment, and train fare home when his mother got sick – but not for luxuries or European travel. Fortunately, he already knew how to economize. After an initial burst of enthusiasm, however, he soured on teaching, tolerating his large class of 45 boys but resenting how little time he had for writing. The boys, he said, were "rough and insolent as the devil. I would rather endure anything than this continual, petty, debasing struggle." Lawrence had never liked "rough" lads, and the only struggle he enjoyed was that of turning his manuscript "Laetitia" into a novel which William Heinemann published as *The White Peacock* in 1911.

Away from Davidson Road School, however, Lawrence (see Illustration 2) was a delightful companion – easily amused, witty and effervescent. He still saw Jessie Chambers, but he was drawn now to a winsome girl named Louisa Burrows, who had also begun teaching in 1908. Her frankness, slender beauty and high spirits inspired him. But no one completed him: no one satisfied his whole being. Feeling torn and undecided, he grew frustrated. The sudden revelation of his mother's cancer in August 1910 compounded his misery. He began to visit her every other weekend.

Transformed into an emblem of woe, Lydia Lawrence died on 9 December 1910. She had been (Lawrence wrote) straight, severe and splendid. She seemed to him like a Viking fallen in battle, like an "invincible spear". It is a measure of his own woe that, a week before his mother died, he met Louisa Burrows on a train and – sunk by grief, entranced by her dark hair, mesmerized by her tawny eyes – he suddenly proposed marriage. She was 23, he 25. He was beside himself trying to drown his despair. In one of the most painful sentences Lawrence ever wrote, he admitted, "I can marry her, and still be alone." He understood his own fierce disloyalty. He knew he must free himself of his twisted obsessions.

In October 1911 an invitation from Edward Garnett, a skilled, worldly publisher's reader, helped Lawrence imagine a life without teaching. Encouraged by Garnett's praise, he worked unstintingly on his poems. But he was often tired and began feeling a lot of anguish, and even dissatisfied love, in his veins. After a November visit to Garnett's stone cottage in Kent, Lawrence got thoroughly chilled, his cough developed into pneumonia, and for weeks he lay flat on his back, fast losing weight. His body had rescued his soul.

He shed his old, sick life like a snake its skin. In January 1912 he went to a seaside convalescent home in Bournemouth.

CHAPTER 2

By the fire in his bedroom, he worked on a new novel, *The Trespasser*, writing it – as he did all his works – by hand. In February he wrote at last to Louisa, to say that his poor health made him unfit for marriage. The old bonds that once held him had snapped. Although he had warned her six months earlier, "I'll bring you nothing but sorrow," he dismissed her without ceremony ... fiancée no more! Later he thought the wrong was all his – and wished he could make up for his disdain. But by then it was too late.

Back in Eastwood – he had gone home after resigning his teaching post – he heard the miners' boots on the pavement, heard the clock chime and the church bells ring, listened to Ada's gossip and saw "liberated" friends like Alice Dax and William Hopkin. But his hopes shrivelled. He was 25 with nowhere to turn – except perhaps to go to Nottingham one day in March and call upon his witty old French professor, Ernest Weekley, who had become a friend, and to enquire about a post in Germany, where Lawrence's cousin, Hannah Krenkow, lived. He didn't know that Professor Weekley's wife Frieda was German, one of the aristocratic von Richthofens; that she was an avid reader of novels; and that she revered writers. She and Lawrence had much in common. At once they found themselves in eager conversation.

On the surface Frieda von Richthofen's upbringing seemed utterly unlike Lawrence's. She was already the mother of three children. Born on 11 August 1879, the second of three daughters, Frieda had been brought up in Metz, in a grand house with gardens of fruit, flowers and vegetables. Unlike Lawrence, she identified more with her father than with her mother; she liked rough boys. She always displayed the bold fearlessness of a man; was rash; and liked to tramp through forests, swim rivers and hike mountains. She was full of courage and vitality. "At school in Germany, all the children did as I told them," Frieda said later; "they believed in me." At the boarding school run by family friends Julie and Camilla Blas, Frieda, though impatient and unruly, studied literature, languages, history, religion and drawing, but no science or advanced maths. What did it matter? She was destined for marriage.

Before long, her mother Anna insisted that she become a lady: look pretty, choose flattering hats, sew dresses, learn embroidery, write charming letters and make lively conversation. Slowly, Frieda excelled at such female arts and finished her education in Berlin as the guest of her cousin Oswald – "I am now awfully glad to be here," she cooed. At 17 she might meet an eligible man, for an engagement followed education as surely as thunder follows lightning.

The tall man Frieda met while she visited friends in Germany's Black Forest was Ernest Weekley, already 33. Stiff and scholarly by nature, he was prepared to fall deeply in love. To Frieda and her parents he looked very suitable. He spoke French and German. Sober and industrious, he had studied at the prestigious Sorbonne in Paris. He was a good man who channelled his passion into his work. When he asked permission to court Frieda, she confided to her sister, Elsa, "I am terribly excited," and added, "I hope that – like me – you will fall in love with him." In August 1899 the Weekleys were married (see Illustration 3). Frieda had just turned 20.

Her marital boredom crept up as slowly as a tide. She had thought her husband and children would make up her whole world. Following Montague, born in 1900, came two daughters, Elsa in 1902 and Barbara in 1904. Frieda was entranced with them. But by 1907 she had met Dr Otto Gross in Germany – a psychiatrist who had married her childhood friend, Friedel Schloffer – and had fallen under his exotic (and erotic) spell. Frieda wrote him dozens of impassioned letters. In Switzerland or Amsterdam, she hoped to rendezvous with him, promising that when they met "the doors to the wonderland of love" would open wide. A magician of love, Gross had stirred in Frieda a fierce appetite that was hard to satisfy. His passion was like fire, consuming his beloved. Frieda soon changed. She was now a misfit in Nottingham. In a letter to Gross she described dancing around her bedroom in 1907, "dressed only in a shawl, while the worthy Philistines went to church!". She had separated herself from her neighbours, and like Lawrence she had begun to pull down the crumbling walls of Victorian prudery. In Nottingham she felt very lonely. Her need for liberation was mounting and with it came a creeping coldness between her and her husband. He took refuge in his teaching and writing, Frieda in married men like Gross, who limited themselves to a tryst. Frieda wanted passion without risking her "position". As her feelings of emptiness and loneliness grew, however, so did second thoughts about the value of caution.

Then a gap. Not much is known of Frieda until 1912, when Lawrence arrived in Nottingham to see Professor Weekley and, by chance, to make the acquaintance of Weekley's wife. Only the shrewdest observer would have guessed that Frieda would be spending her next Christmas in Italy.

Chapter 3
Paradise

Exiled in the sunny paradise of Italy, Lawrence and Frieda spent much of the winter in delicious reminiscence. Both savoured anecdotes of the past. They also loved walking along the narrow streets of Gargnano; buying cauliflower and goat meat at the market; boating in the lake that dropped and opened like a blue fan below their spacious apartment; and, beside the clear streams, gathering wild Christmas roses, "white and wonderful beyond belief". In the mountains above them, at the end of a winding mule-track, pretty villages such as San Gaudenzio drew the Lawrences to a perfect day's ramble. The chance that they would part was "unthinkable", Frieda said. More and more, she added, "Lawrence and I have the deep feeling of love".

But as Easter 1913 approached, Frieda could stand her wretched dilemma no longer. "I do feel like bursting sometimes about the children," she wailed. They weren't allowed to write to her. No one communicated their pain. Worse, no one contained Ernest Weekley's rage. As each fresh letter arrived, Frieda's frustration intensified – she could see them at Easter, she could not; maybe in August, maybe not; perhaps in Baden-Baden, then not. In the divorce suit which Weekley initiated, Lawrence winced when the British consul appeared on their Gargnano doorstep in March, with an official document declaring Bert Lawrence a "co-respondent" who had "*habitually* committed adultery".

Their happiness wilted with the Christmas roses. Paradise was slipping through their fingers.

These stresses shadowed their love. The frictional but joyful infatuation that had delighted them modulated into the ease and comfort of stable routines, edged with rivalry. A warning flared in a letter Lawrence wrote to his favourite sister, Ada, welcoming "your support just now against Frieda", who had coaxed from Ada proof of how "difficult and unpleasant" he could be. For two people who expressed their feelings so openly, marital friction sparked easily. But these struggles for power were eclipsed when, because of the imminent heat, they left Gargnano and – after visiting Germany – reached England. They went straight to the Cearne, Edward Garnett's cosy stone cottage. Socially they felt so insecure that Lawrence alerted Garnett's housekeeper that, despite their aberrant union, Frieda "must be [called] Mrs Lawrence". It is hard to comprehend their fragile position without the knowledge that in the whole of 1913 aggrieved parties filed only a thousand divorce petitions in all of England and Wales. Indeed, Lawrence could not take Frieda to Eastwood, even for Ada's wedding in August; within his family, Ada alone knew of her brother's affair. Nor could Frieda return to Nottingham. In July, Ernest Weekley, wary of her impending arrival, sought a restraining order to bar her from visiting the children.

The Lawrences did what anyone would do. On reaching England and taking a small flat in Margate, they made friends mostly with people like themselves who willingly defied convention. Chief among them were an impressive young couple – highly accomplished in their art; as literate as anyone they had ever met; and as liberated as Edward Garnett, who kept a mistress. The couple were Katherine Mansfield and John Middleton Murry (see Illustration 4). Having emigrated from New Zealand, Katherine, aged 24, satirical and sly in temperament, wrote elegant short stories, had briefly been married, and from her father received an allowance of £120 a year. Chic and exquisitely dressed, she appeared lovely and vulnerable but underneath was as hard as a diamond. Frieda thought her divine. "Jack" Murry, Katherine's boyfriend, was a soft, insecure lad of 23, working-class like the young Lawrence, square-jawed and good-looking, smart and industrious – yet without much depth of feeling. He had left Oxford with a second-class degree. Assisted by Katherine (whom Frieda thoughtfully called "Mrs Murry"), he had started a magazine, the *Blue Review*, to which Lawrence had contributed. The foursome met in July and were an instant success, riding on a bus to have lunch in Soho, amazed by all their common ground. At once Lawrence demonstrated his uncanny powers of perception. "In an astonishingly short time," Murry wrote, "he knew all about me." Katherine helped Frieda greet her children as they left school in the afternoons. When the Weekleys objected to such overtures, Katherine kindly delivered Frieda's handwritten notes. She was an ally.

The Lawrences' five-month sojourn in Germany and England had been stimulating and rewarding. Frieda had recognized afresh Lawrence's startling originality as an artist – "he is so much more than one at first thinks [...] he'll go far", she told her sister Else. However, Italy beckoned. Compared with England, Italy was sunny and yielding; its landscape, people, and climate suited the Lawrences perfectly. Edgar Jaffe, Else's gentle and tolerant husband, a professor at the University of Munich now estranged from his wife, had come to Lerici on the Italian coast, bringing along his own unconventional friend, "a sweet girl from the slums", as Frieda described her. There, on 30 September, the Lawrences joined him. Together, they found a modest fisherman's bungalow in the village of Fiascherino, between Genoa and Florence. They delighted in the four-roomed cottage, set in a vineyard and framed by tall pine trees overlooking a blue bay, where, Frieda wrote, "the Mediterranean comes in and pitches itself over boulders – quite unbelievable". Braced by the challenge to her healthy animal spirits, Frieda was thrilled by the freedom that Italy offered. "This winter," she told Else, "I want to translate and write and paint and swim and fish and row – and what else does one want?"

The happiness that empowered Lawrence and Frieda slowly expressed itself as Lawrence brooded over how to "use" the unconscious forces to which he believed Frieda now linked him. These forces lay so far below the surface, they were almost inaccessible. Then again, Lawrence was looking for a way to exonerate Frieda's untrammelled passion – but how? At this time, artists all over Europe were bending old forms into new. In 1910, for instance, Georges Braque, in a renowned cubist painting, pulled apart a violin and a pitcher and set them on colliding planes. Lawrence too was swept along on the wave of experiment.

Basking in the balmy Italian weather of Fiascherino, he began in earnest on "The Sisters", the big novel he was sure he could write. Choosing as his main character young Ursula Brangwen, he used the critical distance that Italy afforded him to judge how her culture had shaped her, damaged her and enabled her to be a courageous woman intent on fulfilling her body, mind and spirit. In its pages he wanted to portray not what a woman *sees* but what her soul *feels* behind the façade of ordinary events. In 1913 this was new emotional terrain which had not been mapped. As the novelist Virginia Woolf said, "The streets of London have their map; but our passions are uncharted." It was Lawrence's task – the hardest he had faced – to lose himself completely in a woman's sense of herself. A torrent of words poured out of him: "I do nothing but wonder what it is like." For her part, Frieda, lying all potent in a hammock right there beside him as he wrote, provided the example he needed. At last she could be herself, splendidly empowered by his pen.

As the cooler months enveloped the Mediterranean coast, the Lawrences preferred being outdoors all day, watching the lemons, oranges and olives ripen in the bright sun, and, if so inclined, helping to gather the fruit. They might row over to Lerici, with its pink roofs and hilltop castle, or prise shellfish off the rocks. "It is the most beautiful place I know," Lawrence wrote. In the evenings the sun made streets of fire to the distant islands; and Frieda, accompanying herself on a rented piano, sang German folk songs, or asked the peasants below, Luigi and Gentile, to bring their guitar – and their friends – and sing love songs. "The other day," she wrote in January, "we were 18 in our little place." They had created a community.

Into this paradise came dissonant voices. "Mrs Garnett is here," Frieda announced in February, without elaboration. Married to Lawrence's mentor Edward, Constance Garnett was a Cambridge University graduate who had won Lawrence's respect as an accomplished and prolific translator of Russian novels. In Lerici for the warm winter, she found Lawrence's disturbing cough gone and his voice stronger. He may have been thin and hollow-eyed, but he worked steadily on "The Sisters". He asked Mrs Garnett to read a draft. Sadly she thought it "sloppy" and the characters' sexual experiences "inartistic".

In the vibrant spring weather, scented with anemones and almond blossom, Lawrence stubbornly began rewriting, page after page. Frieda helped him. She pulled up vivid experiences from her own past – how she had planted seed potatoes, rowed a boat and learned to swim. Most important, she gave Lawrence confidence when both Garnetts turned caustic about his new work. She was its midwife. She saw what Lawrence alone had seen – that he was fusing the religious impulses of his childhood with the mysteries of the unconscious. These mysteries Frieda helped him discover. What Lawrence wrote about Ursula Brangwen perfectly described Frieda: "To be [her]self was a supreme, gleaming triumph of infinity." As the Lawrences collaborated on his new novel – Frieda its fierce champion, Lawrence shaping what lay deep inside him – he presented Frieda to the world. She was the glorious, gifted, imperious female whom Otto Gross had cherished years earlier. Breaking the old patriarchal mould, Lawrence had aimed, he said, to make art more fully "the joint work of man and woman". Little wonder that Frieda was proud.

Lawrence finished his novel in May 1914. Following Frieda's suggestion, he retitled it *The Rainbow*, then sent it to the London publisher Methuen who, compared with Duckworth, offered better financial terms – an astounding £300. The Lawrences escaped the Italian heat, Frieda going to Baden-Baden to see her family while Lawrence walked across the Swiss Alps to Heidelberg, where Frieda joined him. They then spent a month at Gordon Campbell's flat in South Kensington, London. Campbell was a dignified and successful lawyer, always elegantly dressed, whose wife Beatrice was a painter. Katherine Mansfield and John Middleton Murry shared the house.

Campbell and Murry were the witnesses at an event that the Lawrences had been anticipating for two years. It took place on Monday morning, 13 June 1914. Lawrence, now moustached, chose a dark, three-piece suit, Frieda a loose, white, flowing dress. "Frieda and I," he announced to Sallie Hopkin, "were married this morning at the Kensington registrar's office." Although Lawrence scoffed at marriage as a mere legal contract, theirs was much more than that. It made a statement of their enduring affection and commitment. It would take all their courage and tenacity, however, to cope with what lay ahead of them, as the lights of Europe dimmed, one after the other, and, on 1 August 1914, went out.

Chapter 4
My Heart is Smashed

When Germany declared war on Russia and France on 1 August, Britain soon joined her French neighbour, as did Italy later. In one week in September – by which time the Lawrences had moved to a small, damp cottage in Buckinghamshire – the first big battle on France's river Marne revealed the horrors of war: 1,700 British soldiers, 80,000 French soldiers and 250,000 German soldiers were killed. That was in one week. Four years of trench warfare followed. As Europe descended into chaos, Frieda found herself again in exile, barred from both her children and her homeland. Though she held a British passport, as a German national she could not leave England. She and Lawrence were forced into a prison of patience. Italy, like a flickering candle in the darkening winter months, disappeared from their horizon. Although wanting to escape from England, they slowly descended, one rung at a time, into emotional chaos.

Their timing was terrible. Trees needed for trenches made paper for printing scarce; prices rose; army reservists were called up; anti-German fervour cast a dark shadow everywhere. If the Lawrences had opened *The Times* on 23 October 1914, they would have read that the police were arresting "all unnaturalized male Germans [...] between 17 and 45" and detaining them in "concentration camps". In Nottingham 50 enemy aliens had been arrested in one day. At this frightening time, good friends were vital for someone who loved people as much as Frieda did.

A few months earlier, in happier summer days, the
Lawrences had been the toast of the London fringe, meeting
an assortment of fascinating people – some titled, some
important, some just interesting. They met translators like
S. S. Koteliansky; painters like Mark Gertler; novelists like
Gilbert Cannan; poets like Richard Aldington; Cambridge
intellectuals like Bertrand Russell; psychoanalysts like David
Eder; socialites like Lady Cynthia Asquith; patrons like
Edward Marsh; and rich, titled people like Lady Ottoline
Morrell and her solicitor-husband Philip. If Marsh found
the Lawrences "very happy together", Ottoline admired
Lawrence's "great passion".

Radiant with revolutionary ideas, Lawrence rushed to
meet the avant-garde; his staunchest ally, Frieda, remained
outspoken and rash. "My country is very strong," she would
say. "I am a German woman, and I cannot help feeling proud
of German soldiers." Lawrence would then launch into a
tirade against the war. "What colossal idiocy!" he would
shout. He hated the herd mentality, hated the war, hated its
claim on those who might start a new life in Britain. Inspiring
his listeners, his tirades gave rise to plans and schemes for
alternatives. He saw himself as a saviour. He fused religious
zeal with passionate pronouncements.

Now he needed to embody his vision. He proposed to
collect a few people who, demanding integrity, would shed
their isolation from others. Two friends in particular helped
him. In London, S. S. Koteliansky, a law clerk and translator
who had fled Russia's pogroms, gave Lawrence the concept
of Rananim, the Hebrew word for a communal life and all
it implied. Koteliansky, with black hair, high forehead and
piercing eyes, valued above all his own integrity. That was a
quality Lawrence admired.

Inspired by this vision of renewal and community,
Lawrence still needed a location and a person with money
and influence. He found both. Lady Ottoline Morrell – tall,
titled, strikingly dressed, a woman with grand manners –

responded sympathetically to Lawrence's vision. Even Frieda recognized her regal beneficence: "Dear Lady Ottoline," she wrote, "I am also grateful to you that you understand L's *bigness*, you must be big yourself that you can see it. You will be such a moral support and help in what he wants to fulfil in this world!" Twelve years older than Lawrence, Ottoline had grown up a gangly, lonely misfit at Welbeck Abbey, just 18 miles from Eastwood. In 1913 she and her mild-mannered husband, Philip, bought a three-storey country house called Garsington Manor. Sited beautifully as it was, a few miles from Oxford, its 360 acres gave it seclusion; its serene pond and graceful elms gave it distinction; and in 1915 its redecorated rooms gave weekend guests plenty of space. At Garsington, Ottoline could entertain the London fringe in flamboyant style, with lavish charades, alfresco luncheons and gossip aplenty. She welcomed anyone with talent. Though she was married, she was, said one shrewd observer, "highly sexed". By now Bertrand Russell had become her lover. A leading pacifist, he complemented Lawrence's radical intuitive vision and lent an academic rigour that neatly muzzled Lawrence's outbursts. It surprised everyone that Lawrence would value Russell's modest vision of the future of England. But Lawrence needed reinforcements.

For a time Ottoline seemed poised to provide the centre of this new community that would weave work, home and religion into one fabric. Lawrence thought her "a great lady", worthy of backing a revolutionary political party. But Ottoline, though sympathetic, represented not the future but the graceful, accomplished past. She was deeply entrenched in her class. Despite Lawrence's great hopes, disappointment followed. After a time, Russell found Lawrence's passions incomprehensible; worse, Ottoline found Frieda jealous and assertive. Frieda was Ottoline's double: powerful, well bred and intensely female. In a letter of 2 August 1915, Frieda admitted that "When we came to you last time we were very antagonistic he and I, and I was not at all happy – I thought

you idealised him. [...] Say I was jealous, I may have been."
Increasingly annoyed at being "left out", Frieda mistrusted
the great lady's friendship. Her eyes were open to every
slight. That put Lawrence in a muddle.

It was a turning point. Conflicted, he grew bitter and his
disillusionment poured out even over his wife: "Frieda hates
me because she says I am [...] a traitor to her," he confided
to Ottoline. Frieda saw what he did not – that Russell and
Ottoline patronized him. Still, taking a long view, Frieda
thought to herself, "Perhaps I ought to leave Lawrence to
her influence." Together (Frieda mused) he and Ottoline
might do so much good for England. But Frieda loved
Lawrence too much to let him be exploited. Ugly scenes
followed. Although the Lawrences tolerated each other's
faults, repeated stress damaged their intimacy. In the tumult
of emotional dislocation, Lawrence's sweetness disappeared.
The Lawrences felt they must leave wartime London and
ensure their loyalty to each other. Maybe America, the New
World, was their Rananim.

Long before they left London, Frieda achieved an important
goal. Roused into decisive action, she went straight to
Chiswick, found the street she sought, and boldly entered
the house of her three children. As she wrote to Ottoline in
February:

> I have been to see my children, I just marched into the
> house, where they live with their grandparents – They were
> such dears – so fine and sensitive though they stood like 3
> avenging angels, "you went with another man, you left our
> father" – The little one [Barbara] quite a Rachel with her
> head thrown back – But I felt their love staring out of their
> eyes in spite of everything –

The visit had a profound effect. Frieda soon arrived at a
painful but permanent recognition: "When I saw the children

I *knew* after all how infinitely more to me Lawrence is and my life with him." This was another turning point. Frieda had come to terms with her loss. Lawrence and his friends met her emotional needs. From time to time she saw the children again, often in the presence of Weekley's attorney, sometimes for only 30 minutes. The visits were artificial, the children embarrassed, Frieda in tears, the venue more like a prison than a home. Everyone felt dismay.

Meanwhile, Lawrence proudly reworked his big novel. The London firm of Methuen, uneasy about publishing books after war had been declared, returned all accepted manuscripts for six months. After some thought, Lawrence, ever ambitious and resourceful, split his novel in half. *The Rainbow* would portray three generations of a family, whereas *Women in Love* would portray women negotiating marriage. The effort Lawrence expended was enormous. In one way, however, he invited the blow that lay ahead. When Methuen scrutinized the pages of *The Rainbow* (itself the prized bouquet of Lawrence's love for Frieda), they had marked passage after passage of high-risk writing. At the novel's centre came this:

> All the shameful things of the body revealed themselves to [Will Brangwen] now with a sort of sinister, tropical beauty. All the shameful, natural and unnatural acts of sensual voluptuousness which he and [his wife Anna] partook of together, created together, they had their heavy beauty and their delight. Shame, what was it? It was part of extreme delight. [...] The secret, shameful things are most terribly beautiful.

This kind of writing, so dark and personal and suggestive, would – Lawrence knew – anger conservative readers. He relished the offence to Victorian prudes. So he let such passages stand, along with erotic descriptions of two women petting. These "unnatural acts" of sensuality – what *were* they? When

Methuen insisted on revision, Lawrence angrily complied. Money was scarce. He had already heard the starving wolf "scratch the door" of the small Buckinghamshire cottage where they lived. While obliging his publisher, he refused to mutilate his *Rainbow*. With Frieda's blessing, he cut few of the high-risk passages ... and waited. One night he dreamed that the solar system had collapsed. The dream terrified him. It was a portent.

When the damp cottage gave Lawrence a hacking cough and a lingering cold, he knew he couldn't stay the winter. A rescue came in January 1915. A beautiful young writer named Viola Meynell offered the Lawrences her cottage at Greatham, about 50 miles south of London, near the Sussex coast. She refused any rent. White and new, with spare bedrooms and a bath, the cottage lay in the Meynell settlement near the Downs. Lawrence soon felt better. To meet weekend guests such as Murry and Koteliansky, Lawrence would walk the four miles to the Pulborough train station – and home again. He and Frieda liked the low meadows and the trees full of birds, and they stayed from January to July 1915.

On 30 September 1915 came great jubilation: Methuen at last published Lawrence's *Rainbow* (and a month later came the American edition). The next day, one reviewer of the book, acknowledging Lawrence's "defiance of all conventions", praised him as a writer of "exceptional strength". But other voices demurred. James Douglas, aghast at the novel's sexual openness, concluded that "A thing like *The Rainbow* has no right to exist in the wind of war." Then the blow. On 5 November, Lawrence heard that the British authorities, alarmed by this review and others like it, had found *The Rainbow* obscene and ordered Methuen to stop selling the book and to deliver 429 unsold copies to be destroyed. Lawrence was given no chance to defend his book. Facing a magistrate, Methuen bowed their heads in shame that they had published such a thing and conceded that it had "no right to exist". With little effect Lawrence's friends protested.

"My heart is smashed into a thousand fragments," Lawrence cried. The novel's suppression drove him to despair. He and Frieda were now frantic to find a new footing beyond "destruction and misery". They pined to sail to America, even to the fetid swamps of western Florida; there Lawrence felt he could find a new American audience for his work. In the autumn of 1915, London was cold, foggy, and hideous with war casualties. The Lawrences were prisoners no longer of patience, waiting for the war to end, but of rage. Their collaborative work had been destroyed. Even though their friends sent money, their bitterness had no release. But when they finally left London, on 30 December, they hardly imagined that the place to which they were going was colder, hid more anti-German fervour, and exposed them more fully to the emotional risks of a love under siege, than anything they had yet experienced. The ship they had hoped to take to America left without them.

>─┤◀▷─◉─◁▶├─◀

Chapter 5
A Map of Passion

>-◄◇-○-◇►-◄

Boulders, big and small, broke up the fields; winds whipped off the Atlantic with gale force; submarines, lurking near the coast, posed threats; and the crusty natives rebuffed outsiders. This was no Rananim. This was Cornwall as 1916 began. At the south-west tip of England, Cornwall offered the Lawrences a desolate new beginning. The place, though starkly appealing and mysterious, pushed them downward, one more rung, into a welter of strange passions.

From London they arrived at a spacious farmhouse belonging to J. D. Beresford, a friend of Jack Murry's. Set back from the cliffs, near the village of Porthcothan, the big house, despite its isolation, gave the Lawrences temporary peace. They stayed free for two months. "I love it," Lawrence cried weakly. As the new year began, Frieda agreed: "It's wonderful, something magic about it." Though eager for renewal, Lawrence also needed to forget the insults of the past. That was difficult, because his rage still festered. Whenever Frieda thought of *The Rainbow*, Lawrence's moving novel, now condemned, she went pale: "I am sick with rage too," she told Ottoline. "I cannot forgive them the absolute rejection of *The Rainbow* – [...] I feel a deep and helpless desire for revenge." Her desire no doubt expressed even more deeply what Lawrence felt, for after ten days in Cornwall, he grew ill with what he called his "wintry inflammation". This time it was different. Creeping up and down his left side came a frightening numbness. He felt paralysed. The doctor who

>-◄◇-○-◇►-◄

examined him diagnosed an inflammation "referred", he said, from the nerves. It was a vague diagnosis. The doctor may also have whispered something else, something that friends had already guessed at: tuberculosis. Lawrence had many symptoms: bouts of coughing, weakness, fever, weight loss. But his spirit was strong. To acknowledge TB was an invitation to defeat, so the word was never mentioned – ever. Instead, Lawrence rested quietly in bed and revised – for July publication – a collection of 60 poems, called *Amores*, which were mostly elegies to his mother and to others from his youth. These elegies, freeing him from the past, allowed him to experiment with new kinds of desire.

In a month he felt almost well. Although friends wrote letters, sent gifts and gave money, Lawrence was breaking loose from the world he now despised. That included Eastwood, where he had spent his formative years. At Christmas he had found his family "a great strain", sharing with them only personal connections – "The closeness and intensity of L[awrence]'s family was something almost unbearable," wrote Frieda – whereas with friends he had books, flickering hopes, big ideas. In March, one of those friends, a composer named Philip Heseltine, aged 21, drove the Lawrences 45 miles south-west to the remote village of Zennor, which Lawrence thought "very lovely". Near it, at Higher Tregerthen, a mile from the coast, they rented a two-room stone cottage. Rough, with an outhouse, it cost £5 a year – well within their budget when a rich American poet named Amy Lowell gave them £60. Lawrence loved the crisp sea air. Higher Tregerthen seemed secluded and safe, despite the constant threat of war and conscription. The Lawrences could live cheaply, getting their provisions from the farm below, and feel the place come alive. They could bathe at Wicca Pool nearby and plant a vegetable garden. In the spring sunshine, the fields burst with sea pinks, foxgloves and bluebells. As the gorse flickered into flower, lambs skipped amid the huge grey boulders; blackbirds shrieked;

in the far distance a ship might loom; and at dusk came the Celtic magic of Cornwall. Frieda loved it all.

Lawrence came alive too. In April, suddenly and intensively, he began to write. He called the new book *Women in Love*. Although a sequel to *The Rainbow*, it gave voice to a harrowing new passion that erupted with the fury of a volcano. This new novel looked at Lawrence's contemporary society in bold, dark, brutal ways. It was, Frieda said in a letter to novelist E. M. Forster, "so *bitter* and lovely and *dotty* at times, but infinitely the biggest thing he has done". The Lawrences' personal experience melded into a larger analysis of a culture in crisis – a crisis not of war or religion, but of purpose and priority. Lawrence took an aggressive stand, for he had observed for himself England's cultural decay and what he called "modern intellectual decomposition". Now describing himself as "a brigand", he wanted to write "bombs" that would rid the social system of its rottenness. He let his new theme – of systemic illness – shape the inspired prose that once again poured out of him. With a draft completed by October, he knew he had written a masterpiece – published today as *The First "Women in Love"*.

Portraying coal barons, titled women, and unmarried sisters who (as teachers) are hoisting themselves upward, Lawrence's new work at first sounds like a slow 19th-century English novel. It is not. In scenes of striking originality, a destructive energy explodes in his language. In one scene, a pet rabbit scratches both Gerald the coal baron and Gudrun the art teacher:

> "Isn't it a *fool*!" she cried. "Isn't it a sickening *fool*?" The vindictive mockery in her voice made his veins quiver. Glancing up at him, into his eyes, she revealed the mocking, blood-cruel recognition of him. There was a bond between them. He saw, with secret recognition, how utterly she loathed the rabbit [...] how she would wish it and all its

kind annihilated. And they were mutually related, he and she, in this secret cruelty.

The language of antagonism and hostility, of dominance and submission, is language Lawrence had heard in his own troubled marriage to Frieda. He was now recording the subterranean jolts of feeling that burst through the mind's fractures. No one had yet mapped passions like the grudge that Gudrun bears the rabbit. However, such intensity made readers uncomfortable. It appears later in the novel too when Birkin, the character most like Lawrence, recoils from women and, to fill the void, engages in a nude wrestling match with his close friend Gerald. It leads Birkin to *penetrate* (the author's word) "his body through the body of the other, [...] through the muscles into the very depths of Gerald's physical being". The language is unmistakably sexual. Lawrence was again pushing the limits of tolerance in order to express feelings that had rarely been voiced. He was enlarging the map of human emotion. When he sent the manuscript to Ottoline Morrell, she read it with "great shock". Where would he find a publisher?

On the eve of this creative inferno at Higher Tregerthen came Katherine Mansfield and Jack Murry, tentative but hopeful. They arrived on 6 April 1916, riding atop a cart with all their belongings. Reluctant pilgrims to the Lawrence shrine, they took the large vacant house next door and, with used furniture, made it comfortable. For a while Lawrence and Frieda were overjoyed. The foursome spent delightful hours together. But a weevil soon crept out. Katherine couldn't work, for the grey boulders oppressed her; and from Jack, Lawrence wanted a closeness that Jack's emotional range excluded: intimacy scared him. After only ten weeks, the Murrys left Higher Tregerthen – but not before Murry, with Katherine's tacit approval, offered Lawrence a bruising critique of his character. At this time, occupied as he was in writing a cataclysmic work, Lawrence was emotionally vulnerable and incomplete. That explains why he called Murry "filth", felt "loathing" for him, and later wrote to him, "You shouldn't say you love me. You disliked me intensely when you were here." Frieda had her own sharp words for Murry's treachery and Katherine's complicity: "To me they have been so mean – especially Jack; wherever they have been, they have turned people against me." The Lawrences' vitriolic response to the Murrys shows not so much bitterness as the shock of betrayal. In the new novel, betrayal is what Birkin feels at Gerald's death. Birkin realizes he must recommit himself to a woman, and at the end make his life only with her. Surely that is what Lawrence imagined he should do with Frieda.

But doing so was harder in life – a lot harder – than in fiction. In life the sensual, handsome man did not die, as Gerald had done in the novel, but lived five minutes' walk from the Lawrences' cottage. He was single, 33, stubborn, sincere, and still living at home with his siblings and widowed mother. His name was William Henry Hocking (see Illustration 5). A rural Heathcliff (without Heathcliff's passion), he had tired of farming. He too felt incomplete and wanted Lawrence to awaken his consciousness. Lawrence met him partway – talked to him by the hour, enlightened him, helped him in the hayfields and relished his company. Like Murry, William Henry possessed a sexual magnetism that was difficult for Lawrence to repel. Evening after evening in the winter of 1916, and on to the autumn of 1917, Lawrence would go to the Hockings' farmhouse, returning home late, uninterested in his wife or her attentions. He suppressed his attraction as best he could – but Frieda, always vigilant, saw it. At first she sought a convenient fix: find the good farmer a wife. When that didn't work, and maybe also in retaliation, she began to visit – by herself – the home of Cecil Gray, four miles distant. A composer like Philip Heseltine, Gray was equally young and equally spoiled by a rich mother.

>─┤◆>─○─<◆┤─<

Living by himself, he was available. Writing to Gray in an indirect, overwrought letter, Lawrence linked Frieda and Gray as a couple who (he claims) "need to go one world deeper in knowledge" rather than inhabiting a "suggestive underworld [...] *felt* between the initiated". This odd letter positions Frieda and Gray in some perverse union that is not "open". At the end of *The First "Women in Love"*, Lawrence similarly creates a couple, Gudrun and Loerke, who together are "initiated into the central secrets [of life]". In both letter and novel Lawrence is murky and tantalizing where he could have been clear and exact.

A crisis had cracked the Lawrences' marriage. Whether either of them, or both, had crossed the line of strict fidelity we may never know: the evidence is inconclusive. Frieda had been unfaithful before, and Lawrence had long wanted an intensely close bond with a man. What matters is that some disloyalty occurred, some break in trust, some loss of commitment. If Frieda had earlier felt trivialized in her bid for recognition, now she engaged in a different kind of battle. She liked a good fight. At whatever cost to her reputation, she would reclaim her husband. Her chance came sooner than she expected, when strangers arrived in Higher Tregerthen on a surprise mission.

In March 1916, while still living at Porthcothan, Lawrence had hoped (he said) "that the world won't stare in at the windows with its evil face". But his fear was an omen. The "world", which he had hoped to leave behind, hovered near their cottage, even under their windows, listening and reporting. In fact, just a year later, coast-watchers in February were stunned to see two ships go down near Higher Tregerthen, torpedoed by German submarines. England seemed very much at risk. All around, fear snowballed into ugly suspicion.

One day in October 1917, while the Lawrences were not at home, visitors appeared. Two uniformed men knocked at the door, opened it, entered the cottage and nosed through the letters and papers – some of them in German – that were lying about. The visitors were policemen, vigilant, suspicious and menacing. The next morning they brought a message – most urgent – to the outspoken author and his German wife. It would change their lives.

Chapter 6
Banished from Cornwall

A n official military order required the Lawrences to leave Cornwall within three days. They were barred from living near the coast. They had, in fact, been under surveillance for months. Stunned by their eviction, Lawrence cried to Cecil Gray, "I have not the faintest idea what it is all about." Had Frieda carelessly waved her handkerchief near the coastline? Had she spoken German when they went shopping in Zennor? Had Lawrence's striking red beard, his badge of nonconformity, stirred up suspicion? They didn't know. On 15 October, like criminals, they crept away to London. Richard Aldington's wife H. D., whose Imagist poems the Lawrences had admired, lent them her one-room flat in Mecklenburgh Square, at the edge of Bloomsbury. They had no money, no protection, no way of earning a living. And so their emotional fraying went on, though in a different direction. Still very much in love, the Lawrences none the less recognized that the spaces between them had widened. They had been swept from shore.

They lived now like gypsies, moving five times in a year: a few weeks in London, a month or two in borrowed cottages, New Year's Eve in the Midlands, rented rooms in the village of Hermitage – Lawrence irritated and unsettled, Frieda adapting to a life pulled out in pieces from a trunk. Refugees in their own country, they were always in motion. Lawrence, still pining for America, wanted to find a fresh audience for his feisty, lyrical writing. Like Frieda, he was set on leaving

England. To that end he began crafting essays on American literary figures such as Benjamin Franklin, Herman Melville and Edgar Allan Poe. Abstract and analytical, the early versions of these essays probe the gap between the self and another, between expression and repression.

The Lawrences' repressed emotions that had simmered in Cornwall went on simmering, but under a tighter lid. In the new balance between husband and wife, Lawrence felt mastered, forced to give up an intimate male friend and bound by the twine of Frieda's greater strength. Their loyalty to each other shifted to a brokered pact, almost certainly unspoken. If Lawrence snuffed out his interest in other men, so would Frieda. The pact neatly explains why, over the next several years, Lawrence's novels turned episodic and disorganized, and why he found them difficult to finish. They reflect his frustration. The subtle arrangement with Frieda suffocated what Lawrence thought he needed in order to plumb his true self as a writer. He needed to express the rising *intensity* of his conflicts. Once the essays on American literature had absorbed his passion, he began to experiment with jeering voices, flippant tones, ironic registers – as in "Don't grumble at me then, gentle reader, and swear at me that [my character Aaron Sisson] wasn't half clever enough to think all these smart things." Satire became a mode of dissent. As Lawrence changed, his protective shell cracked – possibly, he thought "cracked for ever". He tried to fit together the broken pieces of himself, but only in a few stories could he do so.

In two stories that he wrote in December 1918, Lawrence confronted the now-familiar crisis of choice. In "Tickets Please" John Thomas Raynor has been given an exemption from military service. Wooing in succession half a dozen female tram-workers, John Thomas, their dashing supervisor, won't choose one to marry. Enraged by his wandering eye, the girls entice him into their lounge. When they lock the door, they beat him with fists and a belt, and humiliate him, unleashing a "terrifying lust". Nevertheless, Annie Stone, their leader, remembers his fine kisses; she would be glad if he chose her for marriage, yet feels her pride rebel. When John Thomas, merely to escape from the vindictive group, finally chooses Annie, she feels defeated and betrayed. Choosing hurts.

In "The Blind Man" the central figure is also rejected, but in a surprising way. Maurice Pervin, married like Lawrence but blinded in Flanders, can no longer serve his country. He feels inadequate and insecure. When his wife's friend Bertie Reid comes to the barn to see him, Maurice – out of intense curiosity – grips the man's head and face, "to take him in, in the soft, travelling grasp". Yet Bertie, who has never physically connected with another person – always preferring simple friendship – quivers with revulsion. When Maurice's groping exposes Bertie's secret hunger and blasts him with a sensory overload, Bertie collapses, damaged. The intimate connection is so raw and immediate that, in his misery, Bertie finds that his "shell is broken". Maurice, however, is empowered. His knowledge of another man's body, though it comes only through his own fingers, will allow him to approach his wife Isabel with renewed confidence. They will find new marital strength. Lawrence's inner self had spoken: what ennobles one person may cause irreparable harm to another. Pain is a consequence of choice.

Equally vexing, for the Lawrences, was the choice of where to live. Having run out of money and cottages to borrow, they accepted the charity of Lawrence's handsome sister, Ada Clarke, who found them a place twelve miles from her house in Ripley. It was called Mountain Cottage. Paying the rent of £65, she gave the Lawrences a home in the Midlands from May 1918 to April 1919. Lawrence would be near his sisters, brother, father, aunts, and old friends in Eastwood. Despite many misgivings, he confessed to William Hopkin that he was glad to be near "all the old people". The war had made him miserable.

⪚⊶⊙⊷⪚

CHAPTER 6

Mountain Cottage, a bungalow with a croquet lawn and two fields, sat high above a steep valley. Lawrence didn't mind carrying water from the outdoor well (lots of people did so), but he needed his possessions. Once more forced to choose, he asked his Tregerthen landlord to ship his writing desk, a big rug, a case of books; Mrs Hocking to send clothes, sheets, towels, tablecloths, silverware; and Cecil Gray to box up the dictionaries, atlases, Bible, artists' paints and typewriter. Since October, Lawrence had not had them. He and Frieda, having stripped away all but essentials, lived now at the edge of an unstable equilibrium.

Half-settled, they welcomed visitors for weeks at a time. In relative peace, the happy summer days drifted by. Enid Hopkin, the daughter of Lawrence's old Eastwood friends William and Sallie, recalled a visit to Mountain Cottage in June 1918. For the evening's entertainment, visitors gathered around Frieda's piano to sing English folk songs:

> And I remember [Enid wrote] the group around the piano in the candlelight, Frieda singing with a cigarette hanging out of the corner of her mouth. And [sometimes] Frieda [...] would strike wrong notes. After several of these Lawrence would lose his temper and scream at her, Frieda would scream back. [...] The whole scene was very dramatic, as we stood in mid-chorus. [...] Suddenly it was all over, and Frieda would settle down and go back to playing, and we would all start to sing again.

The evening's entertainment included this spat. It shows how quickly Lawrence and Frieda sparred over a trifle. Frieda cared little for precision or discipline; the ash from her cigarette probably drifted over the piano keys. She might "scream back" to defend herself – and in doing so appear rude – but Lawrence admired her even as he scolded. Later that year (she wrote), when "Lawrence's soul seem[ed] one big curse", he jeered at her perfumed cigarettes. The

>━◆─◆──○──◆─◆─<

42

"curse" on his soul sometimes ensnared her too. A chafing of temperaments now defined the Lawrences' marriage.

By June 1918, although America had joined the war and boosted the Allies' military power, hardships continued. Rationing of bread had been imposed in 1917, and early in 1918 meat, sugar and butter were added; Lawrence had welcomed a gift of butter as "a great kindness, for I sicken at margarine". In March the Germans had shoved back the front line and used railway guns to shell Paris, with relentless success. In all, the loss of life was horrific – close to 700,000 dead in Britain alone. Lawrence's first cousin Hedley Berry had been killed in October 1917. Rupert Brooke, a poet friend of the Lawrences, had died on his way to Gallipoli. Once David Lloyd George had stepped up recruiting of British civilians, Lawrence himself had been examined – in July 1916 (rejected), in June 1917 (grade C3), and again in September 1918 (Grade 3, sedentary work). Ada's husband Eddie Clarke had served in the Marines, and Lawrence's sister Emily's soldier husband had been in hospital. "It was," Lawrence judged, "a vile sick winter for us all."

Yet the winds of war were shifting. As American soldiers poured into Europe, German morale crumbled. A series of defeats followed. On 11 November 1918 the armistice, at last signed, held open a welcome door into the future. "I long to begin life afresh, in a new country," Lawrence wrote. With the stress of war and illness and the burden of Ada's charity, it is no surprise that the emotional fraying of the Lawrences' marriage continued. In January an outbreak of influenza hit the Midlands. Before long, Lawrence succumbed, feeling so sick he was frightened. "I have been miserably ill with the Flu and its complications," he wrote to Lady Cynthia Asquith in March 1919. For a month he could not leave his bed.

Frictions now intensified. On 14 March Lawrence, assessing the emotional scars of his illness, wrote bitterly to Koteliansky, "I am not going to be left to Frieda's tender mercies until I am well again. She really is a devil – and I feel as if I would part from her for ever – let her go alone to Germany, while I take another road. [...] I really could leave her now, without a pang, I believe." In this outburst to Koteliansky – who disliked Frieda – Lawrence's animus comes as no surprise. It measures the strain of being sick as well as the couple's isolation.

Alarmed at her brother's plunge into illness, Ada insisted that he stay with her in Ripley. Too sick to argue, he acquiesced and left Mountain Cottage. But a proud, headstrong woman like Frieda believed that Lawrence had engaged in sabotage – and did not hide her anger. If she had earlier "screamed" at Lawrence, she would have yelled at Ada too, about her interference. Worse, unable even to take walks till April, Lawrence realized that he could not make the trip to Germany. Frieda was therefore caught between her obligation to Ada, who paid the rent and often provided food, and her own assertive independence, which pointed her toward Germany. The winter had been bitterly cold; Lawrence's soul was still a curse; and the marriage had endured exceptional stress. Frieda's buoyant good spirits collapsed.

Eager to escape Mountain Cottage, the Lawrences left in April for Chapel Farm Cottage, to which they had often repaired. Located in the village of Hermitage, 75 miles west of London, the cottage, belonging to a dear friend, Dollie Radford, lay in soft, inviting woods, where spring had arrived. Partly because the Lawrences were by now slowly regaining their vitality, they were invited to a farm nearby, managed by two young cousins, Cecily Lambert and Violet Monk. The Lawrences enlivened the long evenings by painting tin boxes and organizing the charades they loved. In August, when asked to stay longer, Frieda requested separate bedrooms, not wanting, she said, "to be too much married". The words *too much married* announced the steep price of Frieda's arrogance.

><-+>-o-<+-+-<

Cecily reported an incident that exposes the alterations in the Lawrences' marriage. Alarmed by a broken sewing machine, Lawrence lambasted Frieda,

> saying she was lazy and useless and sat around while we did all the work. He then ordered her to clean our kitchen floor. [...] To our amazement she burst into tears and proceeded to work on it, [...] bitterly resentful at having to do such a menial task quite beneath the daughter of a baron, at the same time hurling every insult she could conjure up at D. H.

Inevitably Lawrence had wearied of waiting on Frieda. Together they descended to a new level of contempt. Emotionally they had been swept apart. No one reports seeing them hugging or holding hands or kissing. To be sure, it was harder now to be in love. Still, all around them, even well-disposed friends must have wondered about the couple's future. What would keep them together? What would salvage their commitment? Or their loyalty?

Chapter 7
Awakening in Italy

>━┥◆├━O━┤◆├━<

The Lawrences did not apply for their passports until August 1919. They were determined to leave England. Their passport photos show how they had aged. Frieda looks heavier, her handsome face now strained, and her suit, cut too large, has a hand-me-down look. Lawrence's face (see Illustration 7) has collected new lines, his eyes are dark and sad, and his tweed coat hangs loosely – yet no grey steals through his well-trimmed beard or his hair. He looks like a distinguished writer. Their years of despair were coming to an end. Lawrence was starting over. Though still bitter, he was ready to break into pale, vivid flower.

When they left England, they left separately. Frieda went to Germany on 15 October. For months she had been ready for new adventures, even though Germany, war-torn and destitute, would not be the place she remembered. Food was severely rationed – five pounds of potatoes and half a pound of meat a week. Her family was "very poor, very hungry", she told Cynthia Asquith. Lawrence, however, hesitated before leaving. He was trying now to reposition himself as a writer and as a man. That meant going south – where he had gone before, when casting off the petty constraints of Eastwood and then Croydon, and discovered the rich creative ferment at Lake Garda and Fiascherino. In wartime England, by contrast, he had felt isolated and emptied of power by having no one to write for. "I must get out of this country as soon as possible," he had said. Now he would

>━┥◆├━O━┤◆├━<

sever his ties to the past, selling even his books. He would fashion a new life.

Before he left, however, he needed to settle publication of two books that reflected years of hard work. Thoroughly revised since he had finished it in 1916, *Women in Love* at last found a pair of publishers – Thomas Seltzer in America (who advanced him £50) and Martin Secker in England; his essays on classic American literature would, he hoped, go to Benjamin Huebsch in America. All three publishers were developing strong lists of bold young authors. Seltzer and Secker would eventually publish most of Lawrence's books.

Before Frieda left, Lawrence shaped a plan. He wanted to go to Italy – "for [my] health", he explained to Huebsch in September – and spend the winter with fellow writer Compton Mackenzie on the island of Capri, not far from Naples. America now seemed too distant, lonely and expensive, whereas Italy he could afford. Italy also meant freedom. Like the hero of *Aaron's Rod*, the novel he had started, Lawrence embraced forms of friendship that he hadn't tried before. Where they would lead he didn't know. For instance, he and Frieda had borrowed a cottage in the village of Pangbourne (near Hermitage) from Rosalind Baynes (see Illustration 6); her husband Godwin was divorcing her. Towards her three beguiling daughters Lawrence naturally felt protective; he had even made them sheepskin coats. Rosalind was Frieda's opposite – demure, helpful and vulnerable. Lawrence hoped that, on his way to Capri, he could help Rosalind settle in Italy while her divorce worked its way through the courts. He might even stop in Florence to visit the kind of man he hadn't earlier preferred: new pathways were opening.

Before catching his train on 14 November 1919, he saw Koteliansky and Aldington in London. Both recorded their impressions. Koteliansky wrote to Katherine Mansfield, "When Lawrence was here before going to Italy he was not like his best." Aldington found him rancorous, resisting the world in a "state of animosity"; he seemed not to care whether he ever saw Frieda again. *So why did the Lawrences stay together?* There were no children, no possessions to divide, no community of disinterested friends to repair the fraying marriage, no pattern of forbearance and respect to ease the marital stress. Yet they stayed together, functioning like two meshed gears spinning in opposite directions towards a common goal of fulfilment, but also towards stimulation and discovery. Frieda was the moving force towards expression. She pulled and prodded Lawrence into flower, gave him confidence, became a muse for his genius. Both believed that she inspired him.

Beyond their creative conflict, however, they also shared a view of life that powerfully balanced them. Fixed in "oppositional" togetherness, they felt disdain towards privilege and luxury. They defined success not in having *things* but in asserting their shared values – communing with nature, making crafts like embroideries, sparking conversation, cultivating close family ties, and scoffing at middle-class conventions. When Lawrence's prose captured the "fit" of their personalities, he celebrated their closeness *and* their friction. Even though he was now in danger of turning away from women, he and Frieda had developed a bond of love deeper than anyone realized.

Arriving in Italy, Lawrence awakened from his bitter paralysis. On his journey he noticed stands of short, shimmering poplars, saw teams of oxen ploughing the fallow fields, and witnessed "lovely lovely sun and sea". Northern Italy fascinated him. The high skies and sweeping plains made him imagine that the walls of England had crumbled. Far from being conservative or puritanical, the Italians were casual, nonchalant and generous. Lawrence, alighting in Florence on 15 November, thought he had arrived at a nearly perfect place, even if it wasn't on the sea.

In Florence he also had his first taste of a gay expatriate community. Welcoming him to the city of high culture were two charming men – a couple – who had found him a room in the Pension Balestra. The burly older man was Norman Douglas, an acquaintance since 1913, now aged 50, who had long ago married and had two sons; his younger friend was the pink-faced, mincing Maurice Magnus, aged 43, who had also been married and had defined himself as "a very sexual person". They were lively, witty, quarrelsome – and fascinated by Italy. Around them, Douglas and Magnus had collected a group who included the fluttering and finicky Reggie Turner. Lawrence's earlier fear of gay men collapsed into wary tolerance and then mild affection. His attraction to men having provided him with little satisfaction, his own search for "bisexual types", he said later, had ended. Instead, although perhaps emotionally unfulfilled, he now depended on the security and comfort that Frieda promised. Before long, he yearned for her stabilizing presence.

When she arrived on 3 December 1919, Lawrence immediately took her for a night-time drive to see the architecture of Florence:

> We went in an open carriage [*she wrote*], I saw the pale crouching Duomo, and in the thick moonmist the Giotto tower disappeared at the top into the sky. [...] We went along the Lungarno, we passed the Ponte Vecchio, in that moonlight night, and ever since Florence is the most beautiful town to me.

Its beauty lingered long in Frieda's mind. But she and Lawrence remained in Florence for only a week, then went south, to be again on the Mediterranean, a source of endless wonder and revitalizing power. Lawrence loved looking at the sea, the sun sprinkling it with flecks of mirrored gold. It provided forgetfulness and hope, escape and peace. "I feel one *must* go south," he had often said.

In their adventure southward through Italy, the Lawrences went first to Rome, which they found expensive and crowded, then into the mountains south of Rome to look at a (far-too-primitive) hideaway for Rosalind Baynes, and thence to Naples and across the bay to Capri, famous for its coastline and its views. Capped with mountains and ringed with cliff-hanging roads and tiny villages, Capri was, Lawrence thought, "extremely beautiful". They rode the funicular up to the main square and found a two-room apartment high up in a palazzo near Morgano's Café. From their balconies they could see ships crawling into the bay, Vesuvius smoking in the distance and, bustling below, the cosmopolitan town, smaller even than Eastwood. They could bathe in the sea, a steep mile down, or dine with Compton Mackenzie – elegant, amusing, and rich – at his fine villa in Marina Piccola nearby. Frieda wrote in early January:

> We had a high time on New Year's eve, there's a big famous cafe near us where all the world goes, Italians, Russians, Americans, short haired women, long haired men, rich, poor, and then the local people came with a band and danced the Tarantella.

Tolerant and genial by nature, Frieda was amused by the island's diversity, whereas Lawrence denigrated the same evening's "high time". He bashed Mackenzie's crowd as actors trying "to look wine and womenish" but revealing instead, as onlookers smirked, "an excruciating selfconscious effort". For Lawrence, pretence demanded satire.

Still, Lawrence's letters blaze with descriptions of Capri's exotic island life – the babble of languages, the butterflies aflutter, the sudden storms that sent the sea writhing. Both he and Frieda liked the place "immensely". On 10 January 1920, he walked with a friend to one of the highest peaks on the island, a hard climb of two hours over dry rock which eventually yielded a view – "beautiful beyond words" – to the other islands in the distance, and to the restless sea below. However, once Lawrence had done all the touristy things on

Capri, he tired. All along he knew that, after coasting around Italy, he wanted his own house somewhere further south. He needed more space, more quiet, more greenery, less of the gossip that their English friend Mary Cannan delivered daily as if it were the post.

On 26 February, with a Baedeker travel guide in hand, he took a boat further south to a bigger island – to Sicily, located at the southern tip of Italy; its sunny warmth pulled him like a magnet. The Greek and Roman ruins in tiny Taormina, on the eastern coast, appealed to him: they linked him to a past of beauty and accomplishment. Maybe this was where he could live again by the sea, in a house with a garden, and, with Frieda at his side, start to write again. He needed to write. Maybe here "the crumpled wings of [his] soul" could unfurl.

Chapter 8

Intoxication

>─┼─◈─○─◈─┼─<

High above the sea, at the crest of a long slope of almond trees, Lawrence found the house he had dreamed of. On 3 March 1920 he rented the top two floors of Fontana Vecchia (which means "old fountain"); its grand terraces looked over the Ionian Sea; to the left ran the famous straits of Messina. Behind the house opened a big garden, shaded with almond and carob trees and festooned with scented flowers. Far above, Sicilian peasants herded their goats up and down the lane, or carried the wheat for threshing. These immemorial rural rhythms were like a salve on Lawrence's memories of Europe.

A few days later Frieda arrived, and was immediately captivated. "We love this place very much," she wrote. "Oh, so much better than Capri," Lawrence added. Here at the southern edge of Europe, he could break free, open himself, pour out pent-up feelings. In just six months, while Frieda visited Germany, he would meet again, near Florence, a special person – and experience a profound shock. Reaching out, hungry and excited, he would discover intoxicating passions that led him into a strange garden of fruits rupturing with exquisite odours and secrets. He had never been there before.

Benissimo! Once again Italy proved fascinating. The hot sun sweetened the Lawrences' tempers so that cross words were rare. The surroundings soothed them. They rose at dawn and relished toast and tea on the sunny terrace. They sometimes walked ten minutes into Taormina village, had lunch at the

>─┼─◈─○─◈─┼─<

Bristol Hotel, looked over the lace and embroidered fabrics that the local women sold on the streets. Sometimes they walked half an hour down to bathe in the invigorating sea, then scrambled back up. In their little blue kitchen they cooked their meals, mostly seasonal fruits and vegetables; the cool interiors of Fontana Vecchia were delicious. When cloud masses cooled the island, the Lawrences might trek past the almond trees in search of the first green figs. In the evenings they sat outdoors on their terrace, waiting for the golden twilight, listening to Mary Cannan's gossip or savouring the letters that the slow Italian post brought in bunches. These were beautiful days. "It is very lovely here," Lawrence told Koteliansky. "I feel I shall never come north again."

Once they had settled in, Lawrence began writing freely, experimentally and sometimes brilliantly. One day in July, sauntering to the old fountain for water, he observed a brown-and-yellow snake drinking alone, "like a guest". Instead of killing it, he indulged it, fascinated as it slithered into its black hole. Like Lawrence, the snake, living "in exile", claims recognition. What Lawrence would once have denied – the snake's creaturely integrity – he now welcomes. This is the snake's message – that all creatures, even the spurned, are "lords / Of life." In this, his most famous poem, Lawrence's compassion for others awakens. He discards petty prejudice in order to embrace what was once unconventional or even forbidden.

In such ways Lawrence was reaching out in new directions – to friends like Rosalind Baynes, whom he hoped to meet "about end of August"; to the gay enclave in Florence; even to Maurice Magnus, down on his luck, who alighted on the terrace of Fontana Vecchia to beg cunningly for money. Then at last the July heat smothered the Lawrences:

It has been hot blazing sun for week after week, day after day [Lawrence wrote], and so hot lately it was too much. I have lived for weeks in a pair of pyjamas and nothing else

>─+◆>─O─<◆+─<

– barefoot: and even then too hot. [...] Everywhere is burnt
dry, the trees have shed nearly all their leaves, it is autumn.

Desperate for a cooler place, they left Taormina on 2 August
– Frieda for Germany to see her mother, Lawrence for
Como, camping with friends along the Italian lakes; then in
September he went on to Florence, to see Rosalind Baynes in
nearby Fiesole – she in one villa, he in another down below,
in San Gervasio. There he celebrated his 35th birthday. He
wrote twice about the time he spent with Rosalind, once
in poems about fruits, once in *Aaron's Rod*, the novel he
finished a year later. Both versions, though coded, tell the
same story.

Throughout August Lawrence likely thought about
Rosalind, six years his junior, in her stately Villa Belvedere.
Alone in San Gervasio, he met her often in the three weeks
he stayed at the ancient Villa Canovaia, which had once been
hers. Refined and artistic, but also an intrepid adventurer,
Rosalind was the kind of sympathetic, nurturing mother
who read Dickens to her daughters, played operatic arias
on the piano, and sailed on Lake Garda with the girls. Long
after he died, Rosalind described their walks and the Sunday
suppers they had cooked. After a special birthday supper on
11 September, they talked intimately, he claiming that "most
people [he] can hardly bear to come near, far less make love
with". He hated, he said, "the so-called Love – that most
indecent kind of egoism". But when he proposed "a sex
time together", Rosalind swooned at her good fortune. Two
evenings later, at the Belvedere, they held hands in the cover
of darkness – "And so to bed," she concluded, leaving to
our imagination all but a brief kiss. Later Lawrence wrote
wistfully, "Wonder where we'll meet next." But when they
could have met again, he was travelling with Frieda. Their
affair, scented with autumn, was already over.

Its effect on Lawrence was immediate and powerful.
What Rosalind did not put into her narrative, Lawrence

put into his September poems about fruits. After each, he daringly printed "San Gervasio". In part these poems are studies in anatomy. "Peach" reveals a fruit wrinkled with secrets, its "groove" oddly like an incision, associated with pain. The speaker rediscovers the beauty and mystery of female genitalia. "Pomegranate" peeks "within the fissure" and, intoxicated, finds it "so lovely [...] within the crack". In lines of equal daring, "Fig" locates the place where "you see through the fissure the scarlet". Whereas, mesmerized, the speaker had watched the snake wriggle "into [his] horrid black hole", here he discovers a final distressing secret – that women have *burst into affirmation*. In the name of Love, they have put their sexuality onto a platform of showy assertion and display.

Then a stunning shift. In "Medlars and Sorb-Apples" Lawrence finds the epiphany of adultery; he crystallizes what his mating with Rosalind means; and he reveals how shattering is his hunger for, and satiation by, a woman not his wife. Here's the essence:

> A kiss, and a spasm of farewell, a moment's orgasm
>   of rupture
> Then along the damp road alone, till the next turning.

The orgasm leads not to shame or regret, or even the ebbing sweetness of sensation, but to separation and isolation:

> And there, a new partner, a new parting, a new unfusing
>   into twain,
> A new gasp of further isolation,
> A new intoxication of loneliness [...]

The intoxication hides his own cruel separation. Even for a man of his sensitivity, love does not follow lust. For Lawrence the act of supreme human connection is an act of disconnection, of a "final loneliness". Frieda hated this

>――◦――◦――◦――◦――<

book of poems, which he published as *Birds, Beasts and Flowers*. It is possible that she guessed the truth, though in her autobiography she acknowledged that "He guarded his privacy ferociously." Rosalind's discreet revelation did not appear until long after Frieda's death. Whatever the case, it is doubtful that Frieda would have minded much. It was Lawrence who minded.

He minded enough to rewrite the Rosalind story in *Aaron's Rod*. In this novel Aaron, separated from his English wife, feels intoxicated by and then makes love to a marchesa in Florence, just three miles from Lawrence's own San Gervasio. Afterwards, however, Aaron feels "blasted", as if a flame had "withered his vital tissue" – this and much more. His response is so extreme that Lawrence had no doubt felt similarly violated. In reaching outside the boundaries of his marriage, he felt not so much rejected, as he had with Murry and Hocking, as – now – unfulfilled and cheated. Nothing except marriage had really worked for Lawrence, and even that had yielded bitterness. Frieda's autobiography and letters seldom comment on the state of their marriage at this time. That suggests that she, married once before, expected less than he, defined loyalty more loosely, and was therefore less apt to be dissatisfied.

From Florence, Lawrence left Rosalind to savour the affair, went to Venice, met Frieda and on 18 October returned with her to Fontana Vecchia, relieved to be home again in Sicily. He was glad to welcome what he called the "lifted-upness" of Fontana Vecchia. Frieda found the place "beautiful after the rain and [already in October] like spring". She was overjoyed that she and Lawrence were once more together.

Some of this joy motivated the brief trip the Lawrences made in January 1921 from Sicily to the island of Sardinia, 200 miles north-west. "Lawr[ence] and I [...] shall *love* it," Frieda cried. This distant island, had it been suitable, might have been their next home. At once Lawrence captured in writing – with exceptional verve and fidelity – the distinctive vistas they saw, the morning sky and sea "parting like an oyster shell"; the insouciant Italian people they met, casual and affectionate, pouring themselves over one another like "melted butter over parsnips"; items they saw for sale – cat fur, dangling "like pressed leaves"; but also, everywhere, the callous Italian grab for money.

Frugal travellers by necessity, the Lawrences carried their provisions in a knapsack – utensils, aluminium saucepan, tiny stove, bread and butter. They made quite a sight. Lawrence was mostly quiet but observing all with a jaded eye, Frieda (he calls her "q-b", or Queen Bee) easy and talkative but brooking no disrespect, as Lawrence showed when, in Palermo, three girls laughed at them: "Suddenly I am aware of the q-b darting past me like a storm. Suddenly I see her pouncing on three giggling young hussies. [...] 'Did you want something? Have you something to say?'" she demanded. Their "jeering insolence" crushed, they slink away. As the narrative continues, town by town, it is clear that Lawrence and Frieda have formed an alliance, a partnership; they are veteran soldiers used to the real discomforts of budget travel.

In *Sea and Sardinia* their marriage shows few hints of strain. Instead, Lawrence captures his irritations with a pungent humour that could arise only from a comfortably married man. The Lawrences' mutual dependence and solidarity are palpable – in their shared dislike of "pears with wooden hearts", a squalid inn roaring "with violent, crude male life", a drunken man taunting a dog with hunks of bread, Lawrence usually *containing* Frieda's natural exuberance. In truth, however, she is no longer Woman on a pedestal, honored (as she once was) by the creative brilliance of her partner, but a wife at the edge of a marriage, firm and forceful, but in the narrative given a thin voice. Despite her energy and passion, Lawrence has redefined marriage as a form of accommodation. The Lawrences' affection has mellowed into tolerance and mutual understanding. Their love now surrounds a mostly empty centre.

CHAPTER 8

Only a few weeks later the Lawrences, though loving their terrace breezes, were also looking far out over the Ionian Sea, feeling disenchanted with Taormina, tired of its foreigners, tired of their tea parties, tired of the masses of winter rain. They were looking for land far away – even the southern tip of Europe had not been far enough. Although Benjamin Huebsch, the American publisher of several of Lawrence's books, would warn Lawrence, "*Dort wo Du nicht bist, dort ist das Glück*" ("Where you are not, *there* is happiness"), Lawrence would ignore such advice. He and Frieda determined to go where they had dreamed of going back in 1915, when, instead, they went to Cornwall. In 1921 Lawrence was now strong enough to go to America. There he would make a new beginning – and find a new public to write for.

"I am very thrilled at the thought of starting for America," Frieda wrote to Robert Mountsier, who had agreed to become Lawrence's American agent. Lawrence added, "I should really like to come to America." Needing a place to live, he had learned from Carlota Thrasher, an American widow he had met in Florence, that he could use her 90-acre farm in Connecticut, two hours from Boston; it had picturesque streams and woods. "If ever you get a chance and an inclination," he urged Mountsier, "do go and look at Thrasher's farm." Frieda too was infatuated with the idea of the farm – as their first big step towards a new life. At Lawrence's expense, Mountsier went to look: "Railroad and trolley fares, hotel room and Ford car on two days' trip to Thrasher's Farm," he explained, billing Lawrence $22.75 for his expenses. But when Mountsier cabled on 22 March – "*[Come] together [–] hurry [–] buy farm [–] cost [to] repair thrashers impossible*" – the Lawrences understood that *if* they had hurried, and brought along a young Sicilian couple to help them, they could have planted fruit bushes and acres of peach trees. Still, Lawrence was, he said, terrified. How could he *buy* the farm? The yearly rental of Fontana Vecchia cost a mere $100.

Suddenly he was unable, he said, to "find my direction". His chief concern was money. Yet he also had to find a path out of his current life. He might, he said, track down a ship, or even a cargo boat, to make the trip. He was coming unstuck from Europe; he was grasping at sails. Now unmoored, he welcomed any possibility. "This is a sort of crisis for me," he confided to Mountsier. Suddenly, Frieda's mother, now aged 70, suffered a mild heart attack. At once Frieda left for Germany. A few weeks later she informed Lawrence that she would probably stay all summer, as she often had when married to Ernest Weekley. "With one thing and another," he told Mary Cannan, "I can't manage my plan." After all his optimism, the American plan was dead. Defeated and despairing, Lawrence now had to decide – would he follow Frieda to Germany? Or go somewhere else?

Chapter 9

East and West

>―◆>―O―<◆―<

The prospect of a scorching summer in Taormina quickly dampened Lawrence's wish to stay at Fontana Vecchia. Despite its privacy and sweeping views, he missed Frieda. Day by day he had got used to her cheerful co-operation and exuberant affection. If his books-in-progress had bubbled out of him like a spring, he might have stayed to finish them. But *Aaron's Rod* wouldn't budge, and another book he had started – a comedy called *Mr Noon* – was stuck too, and would be abandoned. Lawrence had cut his ties to Europe without a stock of fresh experience to empower his imagination. By always escaping from his past, he was forced to invent the future. Every tomorrow became a challenge. "I […] mustn't look back," he told Frieda's mother, who was recovering in Germany. At Fontana Vecchia he sat all alone in the rain, so far off his spiritual course that he even considered going to Palestine.

However dampened, he didn't sit long. In April he wandered to Palermo, Capri, Rome and then Florence before he embarked on a "devil of a journey" to Germany. He had enough distance from Frieda to make him long for her again. He also longed (as she did) to discover a culture whose vital impulses had not yet been shackled. While visiting Capri, he had met an American couple – they were Frieda's age – named Earl and Achsah Brewster (see Illustration 8). Their immense calm stirred his interest. Hidden in a kink of fate was a surprising fact: ten years earlier the Brewsters had lived

>―◆>―O―<◆―<

at Fontana Vecchia. The two families were connected by the house. It was the Brewsters, not Frieda, who gave Lawrence the clue to his future. The call of America, almost irresistible in 1915, was now revived but in a strange twist.

Serene, strait-laced and thoughtful, the Brewsters were very different from the Lawrences' other friends – from the gossipy Mary Cannan, the salty-tongued Norman Douglas, the parasitic Maurice Magnus and the meticulous Robert Mountsier. The Brewsters were painters, living on a small inheritance, whose spiritual life was their prized possession. They lived for their art, which had flowered triumphantly in Italy. They painted animals, Aphrodite, the Crucifixion, the Madonna, the Buddha – and their young daughter Harwood, who travelled with them. To Lawrence, the Brewsters were noble and generous. They calmed rather than stoked his intensity. Yet with them he was witty and spontaneous; he told anecdotes (Earl remembered) "with a light tactful touch". Deeply reverent, Earl had won Lawrence's respect. He drew out Lawrence's humanity as no one else did.

In Germany the extended visit from Frieda and then Lawrence had benefited everyone: Anna von Richthofen mended, and Lawrence worked in the woods not far from her retirement home, at last finishing *Aaron's Rod*. On its completion, he and Frieda hiked through the Black Forest, sometimes 15 miles a day, then crossed Lake Constance and took a train to Innsbruck. This time, however, their adventure – unlike the one in 1912 – had lost its glamour. Accompanied partway by his humourless agent, Robert Mountsier, they eventually reached the Austrian villa of Frieda's chic younger sister, Johanna, her husband Max and their two children, almost grown. (One wonders whether Frieda's three teenaged children could have joined the family gathering.) The villa was located on a small lake near Salzburg. The family *ménage* often went bathing, boating and riding in a pony trap. On 29 July they all travelled to an impressive glacier that offered Lawrence an exotic setting for a fine novella he called "The Captain's Doll". This story creates a portrait of the Lawrences' marriage from the perspective of a middle-aged man like Lawrence who must start his life over.

The story embraces a new attitude to love and loyalty. After Lawrence's affair with Rosalind Baynes, he developed an aversion to romantic love. In June he had urged fellow novelist Evelyn Scott to cast off "love" and embrace "power". "Why not," he urged, "spit in the eye of love?" And that is the new story's aim. Alexander Hepburn, an army captain who has left his wife in Scotland, pursues an unmarried woman named Hannele, a penniless Austrian countess, reduced after the war to making and selling dolls (including one of Hepburn). But theirs is no simple courtship. The forsaken wife suddenly appears in Germany, parading her foolish vanity (she is a friendly caricature of Mary Cannan). Before she can rescue her husband from Hannele's grasp, she falls from a hotel window and dies.

Unexpectedly the captain goes into mourning. He shrinks from Hannele, his emotions paralysed. When he thinks of his former willing subservience to his wife, he "shudder[s]" to think of enduring "such love again", for in his marriage he had become just a "doll", pleasuring his wife. He would not repeat the experience. His decision leaves him – as it did Lawrence – emotionally stranded between a revulsion and a need. He hated love but wanted what loyalty might offer.

Months later, when the Captain meets Hannele again near her lakeside villa, he knows she is the woman he wants and needs. She is attractive, secure, independent and outspoken. Then Lawrence does a strange thing: he uses their journey to a glacier to test their relationship. Stage by stage, from boat to automobile to glacier, their journey exposes their essential selves, uncovering the silent hostility they have all along been hiding:

>―◆>―0―<◆>―<

She turned with a flash. [...]
"If you don't like [the glacier]," she said, rather jeering,
   "why ever did you come?"
"I had to try," he said.
"And if you don't like it," she said, "why should you try
   to spoil it for me?"
"I hate it," he answered.

Against this current of antagonism, Hannele realizes that
Hepburn wants power over her. She turns from the glacier
and ignores his brave and triumphant ascent. This crisis
of separation – she demands he come down; he will not
– is the point of the story. A man and a woman, neither
young nor idealistic, wrest a bittersweet accommodation
out of their joint irritation. Hannele offers Hepburn a
limited sort of love – what he can accept without yielding
his self-respect. "I want a woman to honour and obey me,"
he insists. Hannele, scoffing at everything "but love",
eventually yields. She will marry him. Lawrence's ending,
although hopeful and clever, is none the less fragile. It
won't take much to unsettle the couple's tentative truce,
in which Hannele's spirit and resilience will easily match
Hepburn's tenacity.

This is the kind of fragile balance the Lawrences had
discovered in their marriage. Although they were often on
the edge of a quarrel, that didn't prevent many fine moments
of shared experience. Balanced again, they could depart.
Moving south towards Taormina, they reached Florence
in late August, spent a month in an apartment near the
noisy Ponte Vecchio (the apartment had a lovely terrace,
with lemons, which made Frieda "blissfully happy"), then
continued south to Capri to visit the Brewsters, who yearned
to visit the tropical island of Ceylon. Not until late September
1921 did the Lawrences reach their beloved Fontana Vecchia.
"The very silence is heaven," he wrote, saluting "the peace
and quiet of our own house".

CHAPTER 9

Inspired by his visit to the Brewsters, Lawrence realized he must make money. He needed, he said, to "cross the seas in the early spring", and go east, away from Europe, or west to New Mexico, near the American Rocky Mountains; or maybe, he mused, "approach America from the Pacific". A vague plan was taking shape. The Brewsters' quiet reserve appealed because, as Lawrence admitted, "the older I get, the angrier I become". His stance had changed – from a forceful challenge to social mores to a bitter scepticism about human motives. The Brewsters soothed his temper and, from Ceylon, threw him a rope of salvation: the source of understanding and peace lay, they assured him, in the meditative East. Lawrence was less sure. "But if you tempt me [...] I'll splash my way to Ceylon," he laughed.

Then came a rope flung from another direction. It too offered salvation. It was a scented letter, enclosing medicinal liquorice, and it invited the Lawrences to come to Taos, New Mexico, and live under the wing of Mabel Dodge Sterne. She was rich and narcissistic, but also thoughtful and kind. She begged Lawrence to come and write magically about her hobby, the Taos Indians, a small tribe of six hundred gathered in a pueblo outside the town, where they'd lived for two thousand years. (Mabel was already smitten with one tribesman, named Tony Luhan.) Physically, she was a smaller version of Frieda, with dark hair, grey eyes and a low, cool voice. Financially and socially, she was a version of England's Ottoline Morrell, with a fine adobe house, a wide circle of friends and a dominating personality.

It is a measure of Lawrence's desperation that he replied so quickly to Mabel. He and Frieda would come to Taos, though he couldn't find it on the map. A place on a high plateau, a furnished adobe house, horses to ride, and the unknown desert at their feet – all of it fascinated the Lawrences. "*There* is glamour and magic for me," he told Brewster. "I want to go." Frieda too wanted a fresh start away from Europe. Sometimes portrayed as an outsider, cut off from others, Lawrence usually chose to go where there were sympathetic people: in Buckinghamshire, Mary and Gilbert Cannan had lived nearby; Philip Heseltine had soon come to Cornwall; Mountsier had joined the hike in Germany; Mabel Sterne *was* Taos; and the Brewsters had made a home in Ceylon. Despite what Lawrence often said, he much preferred a small community of friends.

Lawrence's letters over the months that followed are riddled with irritation – with the weather, tea parties, sham of all sorts, publishers both American and British, England's doom. His charity disappears. His letters reflect a deeply felt indecision, even as he laboured, almost every day, to shape two important volumes of short fiction, including many stories that were new, and to compose a masterfully acerbic account of Maurice Magnus, the ultimate con man (by this time a suicide). Conditions were right for good work. At this time Lawrence commanded prodigious imaginative energy; his powers of concentration amazed all who had watched him at work. Frieda, acknowledging that he had spent the whole summer with her family, did not intrude: she owed him a peaceful winter. At Fontana Vecchia he had come to love his view of the Ionian Sea, the living room stayed warm all winter, the beloved almond trees blossomed early and the friendly neighbourhood walks intrigued him.

Still, he had made a decision. He was leaving. He needed only to find a ship to New Orleans, or (despicable thought!) to New York City. Although he had only a little money in England, Mountsier had reported $1,800 in American earnings, including $800 from Benjamin Huebsch's US edition of *The Rainbow*. It wasn't much for two travellers, unless they were masters of economy. But they were – as their trip to Sardinia had proved.

Suddenly Lawrence couldn't go to America. He had changed his mind. "Oh God," he cried to Brewster. "I am so ridiculous, wavering between east and west." Frieda told Mabel that he "doesn't feel strong enough [for America]!".

CHAPTER 9

In truth, Lawrence had no secure landing in America, no cushion of comfort, no close friends, no one who understood him. Wasn't America just a raw version of Europe? Why go there? Instead, a deep impulse propelled him to book two berths on the *S. S. Osterley*, a ship of the Orient Line which held 1,300 passengers and would be heading east. By 20 February 1922, Lawrence and Frieda, in a whirl of activity, had packed four big trunks and numerous boxes for the voyage. The ship would depart from Naples six days later. If the Lawrences meant to have a grand world adventure, they would be on board.

Chapter 10
Assorted Animals

⊳┄◀▸┄○┄◂▸┄◅

Lawrence had booked second-class cabins to Colombo, the main port of Ceylon, where the Brewsters had arrived in October. Ceylon, a large tropical island off the southern coast of India (it was renamed Sri Lanka in 1972), boasted large plantations of tea, rubber and cocoa. Earl Brewster had described verdant jungles, breadfruit and palm trees, grey elephants and dark-skinned natives. When these enticing images came into emotional focus, Lawrence and Frieda realized they were happiest when encountering a new location and discovering its exotic life. In 1922 travel gave them a way to recover their intimacy, and it released them from the perplexing burden of being "too much married".

Their needs had changed. Earlier they had searched for the mystery of relationship; now they sought the mystery of location. "We honestly had no idea," Frieda wrote to her mother in May, "that we'd want to go farther than Ceylon, and now we're rolling round the world." When the ship left Europe, it took the Lawrences to a land where they had no roots, attachments or complex past. In "The Captain's Doll" Alexander Hepburn, his mourning ended, buries his painful past. He crosses the lake to find a new life with Hannele. The Lawrences were similar. The transition came in their two-week journey on the *Osterley*. The sounds, smells and sights they encountered were so exotic as to seem like dream images – the beggars in Port Said, Egypt; old men with clay

⊳┄◀▸┄○┄◂▸┄◅

chibouks; the long Suez Canal cut through the desert; the famous Mount Sinai, towering above the Red Sea, where God gave Moses the Ten Commandments; the superb sunsets, gilded with pink and pale lime; the fish leaping on silver wings beside the ship. "The voyage is rather lovely really," Lawrence acknowledged to Norman Douglas. "I'm so glad we came this way."

When Earl Brewster met Lawrence and Frieda at the wharf in Colombo on 13 March, their island initiation began. He drove them to his hilltop house overlooking Kandy Lake. Inside, the zinc roof magnified nature's sounds, while outside, the jungle, pulsing with life, crept towards the house's wide veranda. Agile monkeys leaped, birds shrieked, animals growled, lizards watched, and strange beasts squealed and scraped. At first these antics of the wild were amusing. But at night the insects rattled; creatures slithered or jumped onto the roof. The constant bestial choir, against the grinding music of the insects, deeply distressed the Lawrences. Worse, the humidity and heat prevented restful sleep. How could they stay in Ceylon?

They did their best to find it fascinating. They took long walks into the jungle, admired the Hindu temples, joined excursions through plantations where tea grew on every hill, and bought cocoa, vanilla and cinnamon as gifts. One evening they watched the Perahera pageant, attended by the Prince of Wales, which included one hundred elephants, jewelled devil-dancers, barbaric tom-toms and blazing fireworks over Kandy Lake. "But even at night you sweat if you walk a few yards," Lawrence complained to his sister, Emily.

Unable to work in the stupefying heat and worried that he had been infected with malaria, Lawrence wilted fast. "I [...] can't stand Ceylon," he wrote to Anna Jenkins, an Australian woman he had met on the *Osterley*. She had urged him to visit her in Perth. He desperately needed a rescue. He was "dead off" Buddhism, soon thought the temples to Buddha "hideous", didn't like "the tropics", by April felt sick "all the time" and, with no appetite, languished. He wanted the next boat to Australia!

If Ceylon had offered a lesson in disillusion, Perth was a pleasant two-week interlude on the way to Sydney, a fine port city of one million people, where the Lawrences arrived on 27 May. Australia impressed them. It was enormous, untamed, unspoiled. As Lawrence's health improved, so did their marriage. Frieda's unpublished letters reveal the satisfying peace that awaited them near Sydney.

Their next move, however, altered their usual pattern. Finding Sydney expensive and their money dwindling, they took a train 40 miles south. Clutching the "To Let" pages of the *Sydney Morning Herald*, which advertised "THIRROUL – Fur[nished] Cott[age]s to Let. Winter T[er]ms", the Lawrences alighted with their trunks and, in the scruffy town of Thirroul, its streets still unpaved, they found a furnished house called Wyewurk. It perched on a cliff that formed a balcony over the Pacific Ocean. In Thirroul they were grateful they knew no one. In a sense they had started over – just the two of them – as they had in Italy ten years before. Once they had evicted the rats, polished the wood floors, cleaned the carpets and stocked the kitchen with fish, butter, brown honey and fresh apples and pears, they felt at home. "The heavy waves break with a great roar," Lawrence told Frieda's mother on 30 May. "Here it is winter, but not cold. [...] We have a coal fire going, and are very comfortable." Frieda, equally happy, joined Lawrence for long walks along the coast and discovered exotic shells at the edge of the surf. Their daily ritual pleased them. After Lawrence worked for a while, they bathed in the saltwater; showered outdoors; wrote letters or napped in the afternoon; cooked the fish and beef the tradesmen brought to the door; and in the evenings took turns reading books, or strolled out to buy fresh milk from the local farmers.

Still, nothing but their swimming and their walks was free. They had spent so much money on ships, and had so many impressions to digest, that Lawrence longed to begin sustained writing. Simmering inside him was a novel about Australia. He preferred to be alone, or with Frieda, who inspired him as she had in Fiascherino when he wrote *The Rainbow*. On 22 June she wrote to her mother, "Here we sit in harmony and peace – don't know a *soul* here." She didn't long for anyone else; Lawrence was enough. "I thoroughly enjoy it here," she added, "and feel that I'm years younger in this new part of the earth." Each day broke miraculous and fresh with the sunrise. "I am stingy with every day," she admitted.

Feeling well, soothed by the ocean's rhythms, Lawrence worked without interruption on the book he now called *Kangaroo*. For details of Australia he had studied the weekly *Sydney Bulletin* and its quaint articles on outback life – rats that built nests, snakes nine feet long, fish that gobbled humans. The novel's main idea revived the theme of stark human isolation that he had explored in both *Aaron's Rod* and the San Gervasio fruit poems; but he spliced into it assorted communications such as letters, extracts from newspapers, and conversations overheard; and out of them he wove a novel of strange political intrigue in which one army group clashes with another. It is still a question where he got all his political information. A week before he finished the book, Frieda read it and on 7 July called it "his dearest book – very striking".

A striking aspect indeed of *Kangaroo* is the way it captures the Lawrences' daily experience with such astonishing fidelity – what they did, felt and shared; and how they fought. Frieda dearly loved the book because Harriet Somers, the character who resembles her, shows so much rapt interest in her surroundings. Harriet dresses in Bavarian costume, gushes easily and sheds "a glamour like magic", but she also shows a manly courage. Most important for her husband, Richard Lovatt Somers – a slight, bearded Englishman – she provides both a woman's sweetness and a man's ferocity.

In one of their spirited exchanges, Richard admits that he wants to connect with other men:

> "Don't swank," [Harriet cried,] "you don't live alone. You've got *me* there safe enough, to support you. [...]"
> "None the less," he retorted, "I do want to do something along with men. [...] As a man among men, I just have no place. [...]"
> "Bah," [she countered,] "when it comes to that, I have to be even the only man as well as the only woman [for you]."
> "That's the whole trouble," said he bitingly.

Although Somers believes he must serve a series of male political figures, he is disillusioned by them and, at the novel's close, returns to Harriet as the person who most nearly completes him. That is one surprise.

There is another. Privately, Lawrence was no doubt shocked that his sexual desire was waning so fast. After all, he was a man who had celebrated sexuality with vigour and passion. But physical desire, Somers concludes, "would no longer carry him into action". When his neighbour Victoria Callcott hints that she would like to have sex with him, he is horrified. In *Aaron's Rod* Aaron feels "blasted" by the Marchesa; in *Kangaroo* Somers won't risk either a failure to perform or its effects on his fragile ego, badly damaged back in Cornwall during the war. At the novel's end Somers and Harriet, like Lawrence and Frieda, are ready to leave Australia and board a ship to America. Harriet wishes she could stay in Australia: "It's the loveliest thing I've *ever* known."

The ten-week Australian retreat from the world had given the Lawrences' marriage a new intensity and a new purity. They had found the right balance of emotion, personal space and quiet. In short, they rediscovered love – on a different footing. A photograph taken at this time shows Lawrence and Frieda at Wyewurk, happy and at ease.

><+>-O-<+><

On 11 August 1922, Frieda's 43rd birthday, they left Thirroul and its perfect beach and boarded the *Tahiti*, a ship heading west. Their fellow passengers were flirtatious and amusing, and included a film company shooting in Tahiti. The ship would lead the Lawrences to the last stage of their grand world journey. On 4 September it arrived, after several stops, in San Francisco. "I have the unusual feeling that America is important for us!" Frieda wrote to her sister Else – although Lawrence was more sceptical. But good news awaited them.

For the first time in years, money began to flow. "Our income is growing all the time," Frieda proudly announced in August. On the *Tahiti* they had splurged on a first-class cabin. In fact, from June to December 1922, Lawrence (though he did not yet know it) would earn – from Thomas Seltzer alone – over $4,000 (about $50,000 today). *Aaron's Rod* and *Women in Love* had sold very well in America, where already Lawrence was, Frieda acknowledged, "astonishingly famous". After the war, as the German mark collapsed, Lawrence would assist Frieda's mother, who was living in a retirement home. The minute Lawrence reached San Francisco and had access to his American money, he sent her a welcome cheque for $30 – not more because of the worsening exchange rate (in August 1922 one US dollar bought 2,000 marks, but a year later 10 million).

Coming by train across the American South West, Lawrence worried that Taos, New Mexico, might be full of artist-colony types, whom he had always found tedious and egocentric. He didn't expect his new patron, Mabel Sterne, to share such qualities; he imagined her as noble and generous. Indeed she had sent him railway tickets and refused rent for the new adobe house she had built near hers. And Tony Luhan – though Frieda laughed that he was Mabel's "latest fashion" – was more than he appeared. He had once been an elder in his Indian tribe, owned land, raised horses and wooed a wealthy American woman. He might help Lawrence discover the profound masculine truths that had – in his friendship with discriminating men like Magnus, Mountsier and Brewster – eluded him. And Taos itself might offer not only an unspoiled landscape but also personalities unpolluted by European decadence.

On 12 September 1922, when the train stopped at Lamy, 60 miles from Taos, there on the platform stood Mabel and Tony, like two pillars at the gate to a new world.

Chapter 11
Mountains in America

On the ascent to Taos, towards 7,000 feet, Lawrence and Frieda sat in the back of Mabel Sterne's Cadillac and, as they climbed into the Sangre de Cristo mountains, gazed in disbelief at the river plunging beside the canyon road, the silver cottonwoods catching the strong afternoon sun, and, later, the grey sagebrush desert burning to yellow flower. The Lawrences were entranced. The air was crisp and dry; under the huge sky, the vistas seemed endless. In 1922 Taos was a village, a couple of thousand people – white Europeans, Taos Pueblo Indians, and Spanish-speaking mestizos. This was the land that Lawrence had been looking for.

Sucked at once into the swirl of Mabel's social hub, Lawrence spent five days visiting the Apache Indians, learned to ride a horse (as did Frieda), participated in Mabel's dinners and "drumming" entertainments, and joined Tony and Mabel to see the yellowing aspens; he and Frieda were "all the time on the go". He liked America's open spaces and rough freedom. Yet he also felt uneasy about the country's hard acquisitive edge, so unlike Australia's easy convenience.

Frieda, more thrilled than Lawrence, loved the house, the weather, the landscape, the Indians bearing gifts of venison and plums. "It is *indescribably* lovely here," she told her mother. "[...] the Indians say that the heart of the world beats here – and I believe it." The enormous spaces around Taos allowed the soul to speak in silence. It could almost have been Thirroul that Frieda was describing – except that, living so close to Mabel, they soon became captives of her generosity.

It was as if the Lawrences now occupied the cottage that Lady Ottoline Morrell had promised them in 1915, but discovered now that generosity could carry its own smothering presence. As their one-month Taos visit stretched to two months, Lawrence and Frieda chafed under the wing of the American cultural priestess. In early November Frieda admitted to her mother that "Lawrence [...] isn't happy here." Yet Frieda was also convinced that the crisp air and clear sun would "heal Lawrence completely" of his respiratory ailments. That was a gift.

By late October the Lawrences knew about the Kiowa Ranch, far up in the mountains, 17 miles from Taos, and were intrigued by the possibility of living there "alone". When they saw it on 31 October, Lawrence, mesmerized, announced that "Frieda wants us to go and live there." The Kiowa Ranch, which belonged to Mabel, was a 160-acre homestead of three ramshackle cabins – pine woods behind, the rolling desert below. Lawrence and Frieda loved its primitive isolation. In early November they stayed four days. With snow all around, "Lawrence felled trees by day," Frieda wrote, "and in the evening learned Spanish with Sabino [his Mexican friend]." But the ranch was still too rough to be habitable. Below it, two miles away, was the Del Monte Ranch, where the newly married Bill and Rachel Hawk lived. Young cattle ranchers, simple and generous, the Hawks offered the Lawrences a five-room log cabin amid tall pines, which, from December to March, they could rent for $100 – the same as they had paid for a year at Fontana Vecchia. Like Mrs Hocking at Higher Tregerthen, the Hawks would supply milk, eggs and meat from the main farmhouse five minutes away. The Del Monte location offered the perfect blend of distance and proximity.

But instead of finding there a handsome, single man like William Henry Hocking, the Lawrences "imported" not one, but two. They approached two painters from Denmark, also single, who had recently come to Taos. Knud Merrild, aged 28, and Kai Götzsche, aged 36 – called the Danes – were friends, not lovers. Good-looking and self-sufficient, they were taciturn but companionable, avowedly straight, and enjoyed making music with flute and fiddle. The Lawrences urged them to spend the winter at Del Monte Ranch, stay in a three-room cabin adjacent to the main house (for only $50), help chop wood, fetch supplies and keep the Lawrences company in the long winter evenings. In the mornings Lawrence would write, condensing his *Studies in Classic American Literature* to make them aggressively vigorous – as for instance when he writes that, although charity appeals to everyone, "you don't have to force your soul into kissing lepers or embracing syphilitics". That is the rough, pugnacious tone he had adopted as being "American".

Then came a rumpus with Mabel that led to a break. For weeks the Lawrences had been dissatisfied, Lawrence feeling pressured to write a novel at Mabel's direction, Frieda having caught the scent of Mabel's sexual interest in Lawrence. They decided to act. Loyalty to each other came first. The confrontation on 6 November had a major consequence. Lawrence sent Mabel a written declaration – he cared nothing for her money, she was an emotional bully, and she would certainly harm his marriage. "I believe," he wrote, "that, at its best, the central relation between Frieda and me is the best thing in my life." He vindicated his marriage. The Lawrences would not be divided. They would leave.

Just as the sticky heat of Ceylon had framed the ocean's rhythmic appeal at Thirroul, so the rumpus with Mabel framed the peaceful winter at Del Monte. On 1 December the Lawrences, using Sabino's wagon, brought their belongings to what seemed like another world. "I feel very different [here]," Lawrence confided to Koteliansky. A few

76

days later Frieda, writing to her mother, emphasized their happiness in the bare but beautiful country that spread out below them, the huge indoor fires burning hand-sawn pine, the long afternoon rides on horseback, the fruit cellar full of apples. "Everything is so good and unspoiled – thick cream on the milk, and as much veal and pork as we want." She and Lawrence baked big loaves of bread. In the marvellous mountain air, she believed, "we have not had a winter when Lawrence was so well!". The challenge and the climate invigorated them. Although they had few conveniences and were often snowbound, they pared down their requirements to the rough essentials of shelter and food. They had no electricity, no indoor plumbing, no car, no typewriter; and groceries had to be fetched from miles away on horseback. It was a life of survival. And yet they made it a joy, living every moment intensely.

After they had settled at Del Monte, important visitors arrived. First, on Christmas Day, came a publisher and his wife: Thomas and Adele Seltzer, Russian immigrants, tiny, well read – and thrilled to be Lawrence's American publishers. In 1921 and 1922 Seltzer had issued eight of Lawrence's books and had, though it cost him, fought off a legal action to suppress *Women in Love*. At Del Monte the Seltzers had a glorious time, singing songs with the Danes, eating fresh chicken and mince pies and apple cobblers, going ten miles to the Manby Hot Springs for a long soak, and at night hearing the coyotes howl by the gate. After a week the Seltzers left, charmed by the Lawrences' spartan life.

On the Seltzers' heels, however, came Lawrence's agent, Robert Mountsier, solemn and a touch dull. He remained a month at Del Monte, then moved down to Taos. He disliked Jews – the Seltzers were Jewish – and belittled them; he was also a stickler for long contracts. Seltzer thought him "impudent" and "meddling". Lawrence and Frieda were torn. Offering candid literary advice, Mountsier none the less always followed Lawrence's instructions and had tried to secure a good income for an author who often complained about money. However, Mountsier soon exhausted his welcome. After Lawrence had listened to protracted grievances from both sides, he agreed that Mountsier should go. In a stiff letter, Lawrence fired him on 3 February 1923. "Nothing Mountsier ever did was helpful," Seltzer concluded; Lawrence reluctantly agreed. But to evict a friend had been hard; it had hurt.

The pattern of Lawrence's response is clear: one moves on to get rid of whatever has assaulted the fragile psyche. Rid of that "liar" Mabel. Rid of Mountsier, who "did not believe in me". Rid of America, which Lawrence "can't stand any more". Rid even of the sickly Katherine Mansfield, who had recently died of TB. These sharp breaks with the past had been occurring since 1919, with one major exception: Frieda. It was she who held together Lawrence's fractured self once he had turned away from love to loyalty: "To me, loyalty [comes] far before love," he had asserted. For Lawrence, Frieda *defined* loyalty. To her credit, she accepted the loss of romantic love. She accepted instead the gift of companionship. But she also knew that her own capacity for love was undiminished: "I know I can love," she declared.

After the long winter, the Lawrences agreed to leave Del Monte. "This cold and this primitive life are really tiring," Frieda observed. In fact, Lawrence preferred the simple Mexicans to the silent Indians or the bullying Americans. He and Frieda were drawn to Mexico, partly to test his belief that a strong peasant life can unveil the religious mysteries of a culture, but chiefly to compose, in Mexico, a new novel. In Taos he couldn't write about America – Mabel had poisoned the well – but he might write about people south of the border. Again, two men – Santa Fe friends of Mabel's named Witter Bynner and Willard Johnson – would accompany them. Together, they would form a little expatriate community. The two men were openly homosexual – like Douglas and Magnus back in Florence, except that Bynner and Johnson were less promiscuous in their search for partners. A couple,

Bynner was middle-aged, balding, rich; Johnson was young, thin and clean-cut. "We might have a good time together," Lawrence urged. He and Frieda liked them.

Far from choosing to be an outsider, Lawrence had invited five people – including the Danes – to join him and Frieda; only Bynner and Johnson would follow. To be alone in Mexico was not Lawrence's wish – or his intention. Leaving Taos on 18 March, he and Frieda hoped to find an exotic locale of unspoiled peasants who were less secretive and more articulate than the Taos Indians had been. After consulting *Terry's Guide to Mexico*, Lawrence had tentatively set his sights on the city of Guadalajara, twelve hundred miles south, one hour from a natural lake. The climate was reported to be "almost perfect" for tubercular types. The Lawrences were glad to be going south into paradise.

Chapter 12
Oaxacan Mysteries

➤-◆➤-O-◆-◆

Travelling by slow trains guarded by armed soldiers, the Lawrences reached Mexico City on 24 March 1923. They were surprised by its noise, its size and its contrasts. Poverty jostled with wealth, savagery with refinement, revolution with peace, greed with charity, political betrayal with religious grace. The Mexicans, despite their cruel spirit, seemed more interesting and alive than the Taos Indians. After Bynner and Johnson had joined the Lawrences at their little Monte Carlo Hotel, they all went to see the major sights – the floating gardens of Xochimilco, the grand government buildings with Diego Rivera's murals, and the unique pyramids at Teotihuacán. They also wondered where to spend the summer.

Two things had frightened them. Bynner had earlier introduced Lawrence to a man named Wilfred Ewart, who, as he stood on his hotel balcony in Mexico City, had been shot dead. At once Lawrence concluded, "it's an evil country down there". That wasn't all. A week after the Lawrences arrived, they witnessed a bullfight which sickened them when the bull gored the blindfolded horse; they watched helplessly as the bloody entrails piled onto the ground. Frieda found the spectacle "vile and degraded" and – with Lawrence in tow – fled. Hence death and horror framed their visit to Mexico. But within this frame Lawrence wrote one of his most evocative and unforgettable novels.

➤-◆➤-O-◆-◆

Both Lawrence and Frieda were wary of Mexico's beguiling charm and found the country "very savage underneath". Yet Lawrence was bewitched by it. He loved, for instance, seeing the dark, handsome natives working under their huge straw hats, cutting ripe wheat with sickles; they stirred his compassion. In Mexico he was looking for a revelation – and believed he would find it. To do so he needed to write a novel.

After the four friends had visited several Mexican cities in April, Lawrence by himself took a train to Ocotlán, then went by boat to Chapala, 35 miles from Guadalajara. In Chapala, he wrote hopefully to the Danes, "I think we may settle." A simple village beside a huge lake, Chapala included three hotels, a twin-spired church, a train station and, at the lake's edge, shade trees and motor boats. Lawrence rushed to send Frieda a telegram: "CHAPALA PARADISE. TAKE EVENING TRAIN." She happily came west. Two blocks from the lake Lawrence found them a large house with oleanders, scarlet hibiscus and orange trees. With it came a Mexican woman to cook and clean – along with her adult son to guard them at night, when bandits stalked the lakeside haciendas.

Soon Lawrence began to write, sitting every morning under a pale-green pepper tree at the edge of the lake. Within just five weeks he had written enough for Frieda to declare the novel "the most splendid thing he ever did". He called the new novel *Quetzalcoatl*, after the feathered serpent-god of the Aztecs which he and Frieda had seen at Teotihuacán. The name refers to the eagle caught within the snake's coiled body. Out of that tension arose the uncertain future that the novel's main character, Kate Burns, struggles to shape.

Kate blends the most distinctive traits of Lawrence and Frieda. She has Lawrence's questing intelligence and intuitive understanding (though not his over-intensity). She has Frieda's assertiveness and womanly essence (though not her lack of focus). Irish by birth, twice a widow, her two children almost grown-up, she is ambivalent about the future, but she is also free to become a different woman and to satisfy her craving for some ennobling belief. Like Lawrence, she declares herself finished with love, avowing "to be in love with nobody"; and like Frieda, she accepts the loss of love but has found no loyalty anywhere. Her soul has begun to wither.

As her quest begins, Kate finds a challenge in two handsome Mexicans, Cipriano Viedma and Ramón Carrasco. "Mysterious" and "not quite fathomable", they reveal an exotic Indian masculinity that almost overpowers her. As leaders of a nascent religious revolution, they point beyond themselves to the kind of revelation Lawrence himself sought. He wanted to pierce the veil of mystical knowledge hidden in the "wild" Mexican natives, whose "wildness [was] undreamt of", Frieda said. Ramón – who is sensual, noble and cruel, but also "beyond and above all love" – is the man who can guide her. Married, he is unavailable for romance.

To Lawrence, now at another turning-point in his life, the novel soon meant "more to me than any other novel of mine". It gradually showed him how to connect to others – not with charity or "self-sacrificing" love but with the bond of brotherhood, man to man, arising from deep within. Spiritually exhausted, Lawrence needed to find a path out of himself, out of his own lethargy. As for Frieda, she had changed too. She now displayed an attitude of antagonism towards Lawrence (which Witter Bynner had slyly encouraged) and could no longer point the way. The Mexican Indians, still in touch with the life of the blood, could do so – but only if Lawrence could weave for them a very personal myth of resurrection. In New Mexico the Taos Indians and their primitive dances had given him a clue. Now finally he understood how to take sexuality out of the body. He would make it impersonal, yet also mysterious and unknowable.

To put Lawrence's insight into action, Kate embarks on a journey to spiritual "enlightenment". Weary of life as she has known it, she draws away to an isolated location (Chapala) where she can learn what the natives value, how they live, and what might redeem them. Awakened by the stirring of a Quetzalcoatl religion, she quivers in response to the forms of music that Ramón inspires in his followers. The hymns – male voices singing in unison – create a "spell" over her, then "tears in her heart". Ramón and his soul-brother Cipriano, both of them drawn to Kate's womanly charm, rejoice that she in turn is drawn not only to Quetzalcoatl hymns but also to its dances, ceremonies and sermons, which "made her tremble all through her body". Kate will learn to sublimate her sexual attraction to Ramón into religious ecstasy. Aroused from her torpor, revitalized, she becomes a female Somers – mesmerized by the passion of handsome men but unwilling to serve, even as muse, their male solidarity. At the novel's end, she understands the full cost of her "Mexican" salvation – the loss of her essential female self. She cannot stay in a country where she will be submerged in male forms of worship. She stops just short of fulfilment. Her experience ennobles but does not sustain her.

Quetzalcoatl may sound overwrought and florid – it features lots of ritual posturing – but its deeper purpose is very clear. In truth, the novel offers a powerful blow to the sterility that Lawrence had hated in both Europe and America. In the experiment of *Quetzalcoatl* Lawrence had drawn a map of the "demons" he so often felt, discovered their fury and, by redirecting their energy, saved himself from spiritual extinction. He had recovered his equanimity and his resolve. He felt he was in possession of his fate – though not of Frieda's. For now it was enough.

Almost done with the novel, and facing departure from Chapala, Lawrence expressed intense ambivalence. He had changed. "I don't really want to go back to Europe," he wrote to Seltzer, though he admitted that Frieda deserved to see her mother again. Frieda in turn understood that Lawrence was resisting her wish that he join her. In July they left Chapala and, ten days later, arrived by train in New York City, then went to a country cottage near Morris Plains, New Jersey, which Thomas Seltzer had rented for them. It was a peaceful place. Lawrence immediately set to work correcting proofs of *Kangaroo*, *Birds, Beasts and Flowers* and his translation of Giovanni Verga's *Mastro-don Gesualdo*. Although intensely busy, he told Willard Johnson that he felt "desolate inside". The desolation soon shaped itself into resolve: he bought Frieda's transatlantic ticket but refused to buy his own. Aghast at his disloyalty, she was helpless to combat his will. Writing *Quetzalcoatl* had given him new strength, and he rebuffed her entreaties. The break came in August. On the 7th he informed Koteliansky that "*she* will sail [to England] on the 18th". The Lawrences still had eleven days to grind out their conflict. Both love and loyalty had slipped into the shadows.

Lawrence had said he couldn't return to Europe and perform the role of celebrated writer. He couldn't "stand on the old ground", couldn't "come with a cheerful soul". But his explanations fell short. They were only symptoms of the unspecified malaise, the crippling numbness, that he felt. There was another reason why Lawrence would not accompany Frieda to Europe.

The reason for Lawrence's wilful delay came from *Quetzalcoatl*, where women assume roles outside the circle of power. For Lawrence camaraderie had replaced love: "I want men with some honorable manhood in them," he had urged. He wanted a new family grouping, mostly without women. Above all he wanted to recreate his Del Monte Ranch life with the Danes. It must be said that, when Adele Seltzer met the Danes in December, she described them more than once as "Norse gods" and endorsed Lawrence's "taste". And more than once Lawrence had told the Danes that he imagined his future with them. "I hope you will both come down [to Lake Chapala] and help us manage [a little banana farm]," he implored. There in Mexico "we could make a life"; or if all else failed, "we might take a donkey and go packing among the mountains". The dream was sad and unsustainable. Although Frieda participated – and also imagined the foursome building a life together – she may not have understood her importance in it; nor could Lawrence easily explain it. In this new family group Frieda's presence was essential. She was the "safety" that protected the men from emotional entanglements, real or imputed. Her presence helped Lawrence sublimate his erotic feelings. In imagining Kate's experience, he had discovered that she could be near handsome men without feeling aroused. It was Lawrence's need too.

In New Jersey these issues came to a head. Whereas Lawrence wanted Frieda to go back to Mexico with him, she insisted on going elsewhere. Often putting out her mother's gifts (thimble, tablecloths, cookbooks, opera glasses) in each new place where they lived, she was far more attached to her mother in Germany than to a new family model of Lawrence's dream. In a surprise move, full of anger, he must have charged her with disloyalty. A week after sailing to England on the *Orbita*, she wrote an important letter to Adele Seltzer:

> I feel so cross with Lawrence, when I hear *him* talk about loyalty – Pah, he only thinks of himself – I am glad to be alone and I will not go back to him. [...] I will *not* stand his bad temper any more if I never see him again – wrote him so.

Both had reached the end of compromise. They did not *wish* to yield. Lawrence cared little about family bonds; although he wrote to his sisters, he never wrote to his father or brother George, and rarely to aunts or uncles; and about Kate Burns he had written, "She wandered to avoid a home, a group, a family, a circle of friends." Frieda, however, insisted on

>–◆–○–◆–◆

reconnecting with her mother, her children and Lawrence's friends (in that order). She had not visited England for four years. The colliding temperaments of husband and wife had cracked the marriage wide open.

Chapter 13

A Ship Goes East

⋗⋅⊷⋅○⋅⊶⋅⋖

By the time Frieda groused that she would never go back to Lawrence, he was halfway across the United States, on his way to Los Angeles where the Danes were living. They were his hope. However, Knud Merrild, though a staunch ally, had no interest in making a life with Lawrence. He was looking for a career in art, not a Mexican adventure. Disillusioned, Lawrence never again mentioned his dream of living with the Danes. When that dream died, another was on the way. It would involve a triangle – but not one Lawrence would have expected.

After lingering for a month in Los Angeles, he persuaded only Kai Götzsche to accompany him south. They moved slowly along the barren west coast of Mexico, towards Guadalajara. Late in September they took the train to Tepic, in the Pacific coastal highlands, then spent two hard days on horseback, catching the train again at Etzatlán. Though worn out and dazed by the heat, they eventually crossed a majestic plateau, ringed with mountains, and entered Guadalajara. In his letters Lawrence rarely mentions his Danish sidekick except to tell Merrild that Götzsche "looks at these broken, lost, hopeless little [Mexican] towns, in silent disgust. He speaks not one word of Spanish, and is altogether an onlooker." Götzsche had become an acerbic, brusque companion who soon found Lawrence "difficult to live with". Idella Purnell, a young poet who observed them together in Guadalajara, judged their bond "casual",

⋗⋅⊷⋅○⋅⊶⋅⋖

without deep affection. It did not survive their next move. Every parting, Lawrence knew, was also a test of loyalty.

While Lawrence, bored, wandered the narrow streets of Guadalajara, he greeted Frieda's infrequent letters with dismay. She would not, she said, come back to Mexico. Her family came first. Back in August, when Frieda had arrived in England, Koteliansky and Jack Murry met her and took her to Mary Cannan's flat in Hyde Park. Later Frieda found a large room in Hampstead, in the house where novelist Catherine Carswell lived, not far from Koteliansky in St John's Wood. As for Lawrence, having cashed in his return ticket he would not, he assured her, come back to Europe. Instead, he insisted, "It's time now we found a place for the winter," while also assuring her that America had recognized Mexico – "and they say it's very safe". Three days earlier, a front-page story in the *Los Angeles Times* reported President Obregon's assurance that Mexico would "renew diplomatic relations with Great Britain and other world powers within six months". But Frieda had other things on her mind.

After arriving in England, she must have written to Lawrence about Murry's kindness, about his misery that Katherine was dead, and – who can say? – maybe about how unloved she felt. In reply Lawrence demanded caution. Give nothing away! he admonished her. "Keep your heart safe hidden somewhere," he added – as if her affections might be at risk. His postcard, surprisingly cool, expressed no longing for her. He and Frieda were still estranged. Buttressed by Murry, who was now editing the *Adelphi*, Frieda assured Lawrence that his place was in England and that, though he might resist, he "must come back". On 21 October, when he visited Lake Chapala and felt "alien" in the luminous landscape, he reconsidered. Frieda's 2 November cable, urging his return, clinched his decision. He needed her strength. She anchored him.

*

>—+—‹•›—O—‹•›—+—‹

In Frieda's life this was a tangled, uncertain time. At first she gladly sought out others. Flush with money from Lawrence's earnings, she bragged to Adele Seltzer that "I have a banking account of my own and feel an important female". She may have been priming herself to live independently; she could not even guess at the future. For all she knew, Lawrence, no longer guided by her strong presence, and possibly influenced by the Danes, might have bought a small farm in Mexico near Lake Chapala. Lawrence could have spared a couple of thousand dollars for it. He still assumed Frieda might come back. For her part, Frieda was very clear about the Mexican farm: "I do hope he won't find one!" she told Martin Secker, Lawrence's British publisher. "I don't want to go to it!"

Farm or no farm, if she refused to return to Mexico she would be alone in Europe and would need her own "sidekick". This was, of course, Jack Murry, who had lived beside the Lawrences in Cornwall in 1916. Unlike the brusque Götzsche, Murry was a vine that could wrap around anyone, be attentive, cling. Catherine Carswell noted his fine talent "for eliciting emotion in others". In many ways he was Frieda's type – diffident, emotionally and sexually insecure: in short, a man who needed her protection, as Lawrence had. Frieda, still smarting from Lawrence's defection, happily stirred Murry's emotional stew and listened raptly to his declarations of Lawrence's genius. Murry had realized, she proudly informed Adele Seltzer,

> that Lawrence was a greater man than he was and how bitter it was for him to come to that conclusion, and how he ha[d] hated L[awrence] – but now he had forever accepted him, no matter what Lawr[ence] did – After all it almost takes greatness to see that another man is greater than you –

Carried away, Frieda innocently reveals Murry's self-serving strategies. In April, five months earlier, Murry had finally seduced a lonely, middle-aged painter named Dorothy Brett, fired her passion and even charmed her with the prospect of marriage. And now he may have shown an equally special interest in Frieda.

So of course did her three children, living in London, awaiting her return. They could now visit her as adults – aged 18, 21 and 23 – and reassess her for themselves. When she saw them in September, she was overcome with happiness. They had changed, grown up without her and become "very tall and like Prince and Princesses", looking "absolutely distinguished", she told her mother. Barby, the youngest, was full of grace, Elsa delicate and reliable, and Monty, well educated, already at work in a museum. Seeing them every week, she knew she wanted them to live freely. Long ago, she learned, Monty had been "terribly attached to me", then felt betrayed – and now must "learn again that I am here!". Her reunion with her children made her life "complete and more lovely than I had dreamed". She had missed them more than she had ever realized.

Unable to predict Lawrence's next move, Frieda stayed busy. After a weekend spent with Martin Secker outside London, she went to visit Lawrence's sisters in the Midlands. Her close friendships with Koteliansky, Catherine Carswell, Brett and the painter Mark Gertler gave her confidence that Lawrence, if he returned, might thrive in London. Murry had generously promised him work on the *Adelphi*.

On 28 September 1923 Frieda left for a month in Germany to visit her mother, now 72. Murry discovered that he and Frieda – already "chummy", according to Carswell – could go together by train: he to Sierre, in Switzerland, to retrieve Katherine's belongings; Frieda to Baden for family visits. Here the story gets tangled. The evidence precludes a firm conclusion, but during the trip Frieda and Murry may have become lovers. For her, this would not have been so much an act of disloyalty as an act of generosity to a lonely man. She liked Murry "very much", she told her mother. Lawrence's plans were still vague. And when on 12 December he arrived in London, where he was met at Waterloo Station by Frieda, Murry and Koteliansky, he judged for himself the intimacy between his wife and Murry – and may have been gravely disturbed. In fact, Frieda wrote later, in 1934, that Lawrence "should not have come [back] to Europe"; rather, she ought to have "[met] him in Mexico". That is a hint, but no more than a hint, that she may have compromised herself in Lawrence's absence.

On his arrival, Lawrence despised England – the foul weather, the lack of freedom and openness, the fawning Murry (still, after eight years, a continuing addiction). "Here I am – in bed with a cold – hate it," he told Idella Purnell on the 17th. "Just hate it all. It's like being in the tomb. [...] I swear at [Frieda] for having brought me here." In late December, Lawrence allowed her to invite a few friends to a welcome-home supper held at a private room in London's Café Royal. Lawrence was a gracious and entertaining host, and Frieda purred with delight. But the gathering turned from a convivial exchange into a test of loyalty when Lawrence, laced with liquor, asked each person in turn to go with him to New Mexico to create a community bonded in trust and support. Frieda, holding herself aloof, said little. But Catherine Carswell, a careful observer, caught the jealous male flavour of the evening – Koteliansky declaiming that "no woman here or anywhere [Frieda was exempt] can possibly realise the greatness of Lawrence", and then Murry spewing effusive love for Lawrence, and with masked malice reminding Catherine that "women can have no part or place" in the lively procession of male bonding. To Lawrence it must have seemed as if the Danes had gone voluble and berserk. He sat "still and unresponsive", likely impressed but certainly disbelieving. Elsewhere he had argued that one must "eschew emotions – they are a disease". He had in mind Murry's brand of emotional pheromones.

All the guests – save one – sooner or later made their excuses. The exception was Dorothy Brett (see Illustration 8), a Slade-trained artist, 40, unmarried, mostly deaf, and, by June, pregnant with Murry's child (though she soon lost it). She had ample money (£500 a year from her father, Viscount Esher), a pedigree (she was the *Honourable* Dorothy Brett), much talent, a sweet temperament and a genuine fondness for Lawrence. She agreed to go to Taos in the spring; for Lawrence had concluded that, for genuine living in the United States, "Taos is about the best place".

As 1924 began, Lawrence (depressed) and Frieda (exuberant) took a two-week trip to Paris, visiting Malmaison and Chartres, and then went on to Baden-Baden to spend February with Frieda's mother. Travel was a quick fix for their discontent. Now distanced from London, Lawrence wrote a very personal story called "The Border-Line", which, adopting Frieda's point of view, is a thinly disguised letter to his wife. Lawrence brazenly calls her "Katharine", the exact misspelling Lawrence had always used for Murry's wife. After ten years of marriage, Katharine (Frieda) and her husband Alan (Lawrence) stop living together. After his death, she takes up with Alan's close friend Philip, a journalist (Murry), who wraps Katharine in "subtle, cunning homage" and marries her, offering her no critique (he is too cringing for that) but inflating her female ego. Suddenly Lawrence brings into the story Alan's ghost (a wondrous mouthpiece) who walks beside her:

> And dimly she wondered why, why, why she had ever fought against [Alan's comradeship]. [...] The strong, silent kindliness of him towards her, even now [in the afterlife], was able to wipe out the ashy nervous horror of the world from her body. She went at his side [...] walking in the dimness of her own contentment.

The story openly confronts Lawrence's crisis. He acknowledges his fears, then (though in disguise) shares them with Frieda. This is one of many stories that comment indirectly on the Lawrences' emotional conflicts. He wanted his marriage to survive. One way to effect this was to make Frieda appreciate him anew. Whether or not Frieda and Murry consummated their "chummy" bond, Lawrence wrote *as if they had*. That's what mattered, and it coloured and arguably affected the rest of his life. His trust in others slowly gathered a mould of cynicism about human motive. Though Lawrence did not hold grudges, he never forgot a slight. He blamed Murry more than Frieda – Murry had professed both love and loyalty, Frieda just love. Lawrence therefore pined to return to America. "God get me out of here," he had cried in December.

But even in America, all was not well. Despite strong sales of his books in 1923, Lawrence had not been getting letters from his esteemed publisher, Thomas Seltzer, or Seltzer's wife Adele. He was aware that Seltzer procrastinated – that he often put off writing important letters – and so Lawrence didn't fret until his American taxes were due. Since August he had heard once from Seltzer, then nothing at all about his American royalty payments. But Seltzer had firmly promised Lawrence that he would be "loyal to you". Uneasy, even anxious, but with no hint of panic, Lawrence decided to return to Taos via New York, bring along Frieda and Brett, and appraise Seltzer's affairs for himself. On 5 March 1924 they boarded the *Aquitania*. The Lawrences had recently spent thousands of dollars. Their fountain of money had supplied Frieda's German relatives and paid for train tickets, ship fares, hotel rooms, expensive meals, gifts, stylish Parisian clothes. They could not afford to let the fountain run dry. The thought of being poor again was detestable.

Chapter 14
Frieda's Pine Woods

➤━┥◆▶━○━◀◆┝━◄

When Lawrence arrived in America, his fears were confirmed. Thomas Seltzer was headed for ruin. In a tight fiction market, he had bet on the wrong books. "At the moment," Lawrence cried, "I have no money at all in the bank." It was a painful admission, though Seltzer did cover the Lawrences' train fare to Taos. That was where they most wanted to go for the spring and summer. There, in the Promised Land, they could live simply in a landscape that might inspire Lawrence to write.

Lawrence was determined that Taos would be different this time. Europe had wearied him "inexpressibly", sent him into a "depression" and made him recoil from big cities. The trip west, which began on 22 March 1924, took the travellers from New York City, through Chicago, to Mabel Sterne's desert compound, where the Lawrences occupied the two-storey structure across from her big house, and where Brett – thrilled to be in America – took the studio nearby. Mabel, who had endured a bitter winter too, at first seemed mellow and kind. The new beginning in Taos promised real happiness; for these were all bruised people who had come (or returned) to Taos to heal.

Lawrence welcomed the hot sun and the singing birds, loved riding the mustang ponies again, and felt his soul thawing out. Even Frieda, he said, was "growing lively again". Away from high costs and emotional temptations, away from living in hotels, the Lawrences could, as the

➤━┥◆▶━○━◀◆┝━◄

snow melted and spring roused their spirits, begin to rescue the torn remnants of their marriage. As they brokered the lingering tensions between them, they understood that healing might take months. For a man like Lawrence, who described himself as "essentially a fighter", the healing was slow and never complete.

Dorothy Brett (always called just Brett) both eased and complicated the Lawrences' transition from nomads to settlers. She eased it by buffering two sparring personalities, but complicated it by treating Lawrence as an idol under Frieda's gaze. Mabel also smelled competition. After meeting Brett, Mabel called her a "grotesque". Brett carried a brass ear-trumpet (to hear better), whirling it in all directions to catch scraps of conversation. Undaunted, she examined Mabel with hostile, questioning eyes: "curious, arrogant and English", Mabel wrote. Lawrence reminded everyone that Brett was a Viscount's daughter.

But the surprise is what Brett became. Away from England and class snobbery, she could daringly reinvent herself – not as the demure, drawing-room spinster that Mabel or Frieda would have preferred, but as an American cowboy. She turned herself into what Lawrence had long been wanting. She became his sidekick – a Kai Götzsche whose admiration and love never wavered. Earlier, when Brett agreed to accompany him to America, he had called her (approvingly) "a real odd man out". Now she wore a wide sombrero and baggy men's trousers stuffed into cowboy boots, sometimes with a dagger thrust into her right boot. A sport for every adventure, she later rode with Lawrence (mostly in silence), felled trees, chopped wood, wielded a hammer, caught fish, shot rabbits and pack-rats; in short, she masculinized herself, partly to adapt to a freer culture, partly to prevent sex from coming between them. (When finally it did, disaster followed.)

After a month of Mabel's organized festivities, which unfolded in vague discomfort, the Lawrences yearned for the quiet, savage beauty of a mountain ranch like Del Monte, their home a year earlier. Still attuned to their needs, Mabel offered Frieda the Kiowa Ranch two miles above Del Monte. In 1923 the Lawrences had loved it. As payment, Frieda proudly gave Mabel the handwritten manuscript of *Sons and Lovers* – "worth fifty thousand dollars", Frieda claimed – which she and Lawrence had carefully recast in Gargnano, Italy, as they explored the first stages of their love. The Kiowa Ranch's three old cabins needed much repair – new roofs, chimneys, chinking of walls, coats of paint. On 6 April the Lawrences and Brett, driven by Tony Luhan (not yet Mabel's Indian husband), visited the ranch. Amazed, Lawrence vowed to move up to it. Though long since refusing to own things, Lawrence yet swelled with pride at what he called "Frieda's ranch".

When the day of possession came a month later, they brought along three strong Indians – Geronimo, Candido and Trinidad – and a Mexican carpenter named Richard. Lawrence, Frieda and Brett set up camps near the three cabins: one camp for themselves and another, higher up the mountain, for the Indians. Frieda cooked their meals while Lawrence, assisted by Brett, organized their work. Despite the altitude of 8,500 feet, he had never worked harder in his life, from morning till night, day after day – cleaning, hauling, constructing. The effort was exhausting. As the sun set, they would all gather around a campfire, the Indians singing and drumming and dancing, the firelight flashing over the whites of their eyes. Frieda admired the Indians' way of making a game of their work – inefficient but enjoyable; and Lawrence admired their skill in rebuilding, plastering, restoring the barn and making adobe bricks for a new chimney and an outdoor oven. Moving into the finished three-room house on 24 May was, Lawrence wrote, "great fun". Apart from the big kitchen with plank floors, Lawrence had a separate bedroom, while the sitting-room doubled as Frieda's bedroom. Brett enjoyed a tiny cabin all to herself. Rebuilding the ranch cost less than $500. Surveying her renovated ranch, Frieda wittily called it "simple and stylish".

Not that Lawrence wasted anything on stylishness. Now that Seltzer's royalty payments had ended, the Lawrences agreed to be "very economical". They picked their own strawberries and raspberries, bought vegetables like cauliflower, ate chicken sparingly and, without refrigeration, pickled their beef. With such a limited supply of water, they hadn't planted a garden. Still, the summer passed in a comfortable rhythm. Brett painted, Lawrence wrote every morning and sometimes baked bread, Frieda sewed, cooked bacon and eggs, and read books, a cigarette never far from her lips. Every day at dusk all three saddled their horses and rode two miles through the woods to Del Monte, going for fresh milk and the post. Mabel's interference, always a risk, had been minimized.

And all summer the spirit of the ranch impressed them with its raw challenge and energy. In July Lawrence wrote to Frieda's mother, "Here, where one is alone with trees and mountains and chipmunks and desert, one gets something out of the air: something wild and untamed, cruel and proud, beautiful and sometimes evil, that really is America." Lawrence found here the echo of his deepest self. This wild, cruel, proud spirit defined a story he had written at the ranch during one fine week in June. It was called "The Woman Who Rode Away". It is a brilliant but disturbing story.

It is disturbing because of the cool anger that informs it. On the surface the anger arose from Mabel. She had a knack for insult even when she proffered kindness. That infuriated Lawrence. The luminous landscape around him could not eradicate his belief that America's spirit, and America's women, were "sometimes evil". The woman in his story, not given a name, leaves an unsatisfying marriage – as Mabel had. Both are fascinated by Indians. Back in October, Lawrence and Götzsche had seen an ancient tribe of

Mexican Indians coming down from the far mountains into Guadalajara, dressed strangely; older and more primitive than the Taos Pueblo Indians; a "pristine race", Götzsche thought. Lawrence too was fascinated. It is to these Chilchui Indians that the Woman "rides away" from her children and marriage, compelled to find "the secret haunts of these timeless, mysterious, marvellous Indians".

The secret she doesn't know is that the Indians have suffered a grave loss of power. They need a sacrifice to propitiate their angry gods of sun and moon. Finding her ascending the mountains alone, searching for their gods, they help the Woman to undergo a transformation from wilful arrogance to complete submission. To them she is not a female, but a spiritual conduit. She has no sexual appeal. Given herbal drinks, she gains transcendent new knowledge and hears the heavenly stars sing "like bells" to the dancing cosmos. She is unafraid of death. Gradually, when the Indians' silence and sexless power disable her will, she is taken to a sacred altar inside a cave; and just when the sun shines deepest into the cave, the priest raises his phallic knife and, as the whole tribe watches, prepares to reclaim the racial power his people have lost. He will sacrifice the Woman.

What startles readers is that the men of the tribe, like Lawrence himself, have rechannelled their sexual drive outside the body. The men are fulfilled not by an act of love but by an act of violence. After the disappointments of the past – Lawrence admitted he had been "badly hurt" – he was left with a residual fury that darkened all his remaining work. Lawrence's love for Frieda had thinned into complex friendship, for in Frieda's soul too, she complained, came "a steady suppressed growl". She had put her sexual longing into low gear. To do so was small penance for her dalliance with Murry a year earlier. Turning 45 on 11 August, she had tired of human pettiness, her own included. Brett's account of the summer months doesn't record a single instance of

1 Lawrence's Family, Nottingham, c. 1895. Back row: Emily, George, Ernest; front row: Ada, Lydia, D. H. Lawrence, Arthur

2 D. H. Lawrence, Croydon, 1908

3 Charles, Agnes, Ernest and Frieda Weekley, c. 1900

4 Katherine Mansfield and John Middleton Murry, c. 1914

5 William Henry Hocking,
Cornwall, c. 1917

6 Rosalind Baynes, with daughter Bridget, c. 1914

7 D. H. Lawrence, passport photo, 1919

8 Back row: Harwood Brewster, Earl Brewster; front row: Dorothy
Brett, Achsah Brewster, D. H. Lawrence, Capri, 1926

9 The Villa Mirenda, near
Florence

10 Maria and Aldous Huxley,
c. 1928

11 Giuseppe Orioli, Frieda and D. H. Lawrence, Florence, 1928

12 Frieda Lawrence,
1938

13 Angelo Ravagli, Frieda Lawrence and Johnie Griffin, c. 1951

the Lawrences' affection for each other; it reveals a brusque camaraderie. Lawrence had disowned love. He wanted it reinterpreted as if it were the sun without heat; as if it were a presence, even a powerful presence, but not an embrace. He no longer wanted to be touched, except by the same cosmic forces that moved the Chilchui Indians.

Yet in the story the Chilchui are dying. Lawrence doesn't say whether the Woman's death made a difference. Their poignant, sacrificial call to their gods comes with a violent but passionate plea for rescue. In this they resembled Lawrence himself. That summer he told Brett, "To bring the gods, you must call them to you." Lawrence's proud, lonely call had not brought them. He needed to go where they might hear him. In Old Mexico he had heard of the Zapotec Indians who had preserved their ancient culture around the city of Oaxaca, in the south. He wanted, he told E. M. Forster, to "see the gods again" there in Mexico, and perhaps rewrite his novel *Quetzalcoatl* with fuller knowledge of their cosmos. He wanted to know what beyond violence – and silence – they might demand of him.

And what did Frieda demand? Admitting in September, "This country has become part of me," she would have preferred going to Germany, but would wait. She explained her revised sense of commitment: "sometimes I do what he wants", and sometimes not. Their marriage still required compromise. Indeed, by themselves, the Lawrences were mostly busy and companionable, even loyal, though perhaps no longer "intimate". In her book Brett portrays Frieda as mostly disagreeable in the summer of 1924; but Frieda's bouts of hostility arose mostly when Brett took Lawrence's part in a dispute. In her letters Frieda appears surprisingly brave and optimistic – saying, for instance, that "Lawrence looks so good". Whereas Brett often describes Lawrence's illnesses (headaches, fatigue, coughing, spitting up blood), Frieda concluded that the mountain air "has been good for him" – "lungs and heart are excellent", a doctor had said. That was what she preferred to hear. Frieda looked resolutely forward. She would neither pamper Lawrence when he was sick nor traffic in words of pity or defeat. Her strength lay in knowing how to let Lawrence, without doctors, rescue himself. He listened mostly to the voices inside him. When Frieda did once call a doctor in July, Lawrence was "furious".

Before leaving to go south, the Lawrences took a long, hot, tiring trip to see the Hopi Indian Snake Dance. Lawrence disliked the crude spectacle, but after Mabel's complaint that he had written too dismissively, he later appreciated it. He saw that the Hopi Indians of Arizona did whatever they could – even gripping shiny rattlesnakes between their teeth – to appease the inscrutable "cosmic beasts" of sunshine, thunder, wind and rain. These potent powers, more like dragons than gods, awakened Lawrence's questing spirit. He nobly persisted in seeking personal salvation. Although America's Indians, tainted by Mabel's special pleading, had offered him limited spiritual nourishment, Frieda later said that the "real, religious, reverent attitude to all life, we got there [in Taos], affirmed in the Indians". Unlike Mabel, Lawrence did not want to save them; he wanted to be inspired by their rituals and their need to understand forces beyond love. Further south he might find just what he sought.

After wintering in Mexico, Frieda firmly intended to return to the ranch in April. She acknowledged Brett and Mabel's mutual dislike, as well as Mabel's compulsive need "to interfere with Lawrence", yet she looked forcefully ahead. In the spring she wanted to grow a large vegetable garden; cultivate strawberries, currants, gooseberries; raise ducks; and milk a cow. "There is so much space," she exclaimed to her mother. Kiowa was becoming the Thrasher Farm in Connecticut, which Lawrence had dreamed of in 1921 and sent Robert Mountsier to assess. Now, in New Mexico, the dream was a reality. Far from cities and towns, Kiowa's stark grandeur supplied a unique kind of comfort.

The ranch resembled other isolated places where they had lived – Gargnano, Higher Tregerthen, Mountain Cottage, Fontana Vecchia – but there was a difference: it was Frieda's. From Mexico, she could return with Lawrence, sick or well, and know they were coming home.

Sad to abandon their beloved horses, Lawrence, Frieda and Brett left the ranch on 11 October. They spent the early autumn days packing trunks, shuttering windows and moving winter clothes to Del Monte below. Who would have guessed that Lawrence would return to the ranch just five months later? By then he was a different man.

Chapter 15
Frightened

>‑◆‑O‑◆‑‑<

The slow train, guarded again by armed soldiers, headed
south from El Paso to Mexico City. Some days later
it jolted 350 miles through the Mexican state of Puebla,
lumbering across the wild, hilly, dusty country before crawling
down towards the huge plain around the town of Oaxaca
(pronounced Wa-*hock*-ah). "You don't know how different
and strange it is until you see the people," Lawrence alerted
Brett as they approached. The ancient Zapotec Indians made
up two-thirds of Oaxaca's population. Short, stocky, black-
haired and broad-faced, they were farmers who used oxen
to harvest corn and sugar-cane, and superb craftsmen who
wove intricately designed wool rugs and blankets. Although
they had slowly developed a culture of heroic patriarchy,
Lawrence sensed that the postcard images of the Zapotec
Indians hid a sad reality. Ten years earlier, rebel fighting
had compromised their co-operative stability. Even Frieda,
sometimes less perceptive than Lawrence, was disturbed by
"these dying, apathetic Indians". The Lawrences' second
Mexican adventure began in great anticipation. It would
end in crisis.

In Oaxaca, a sleepy town of 30,000, the Lawrences, with
Brett, stepped off the train on 9 November 1924, Lawrence
wearing a black-and-white checked suit, paired with a tie
from Frieda's mother, Frieda wearing a cotton dress and a
plain bowler hat. The town, which seemed peaceful and quiet,
offered a perfect climate. The sun shone brightly all day. At

>‑◆‑O‑◆‑‑<

5,000 feet, the elevation was "just right" for Lawrence's sore chest. The Lawrences settled into the Hotel Francia, near both the main square and the covered market, but they soon moved to the edge of town – to an adobe house, solid and flat-roofed, on Avenida Pino Suárez, with a handsome wide veranda facing an enclosed garden. They could eat all their meals outdoors. In 1995 the owner proudly gestured to the foot-thick walls: *"¡Mire! Pero mire las paredes: ¡tan gruesas que nunca se han derribado en un temblor!"* ("Look! Just look at the walls: so thick they've never crumbled in an earthquake!")

The Lawrences always preferred to experience a place at first hand. When they wanted an excursion, they would take a mule-drawn tram to the crowded covered market. There they perused the local pottery, black and gleaming; the heavy silver jewellery; pyramids of limes and oranges; boldly designed serapes; roses in profusion; even live chickens. Smells and colours mixed with dozens of dialects. Sometimes they would sit in the main square, waiting for a band to play or a silent film to start. Despite rumours of violence, they would walk to an Indian village like Huayapan, their Zapotec servant Rosalino carrying their picnic basket. Because Frieda and Brett had learned so little Spanish, and because Rosalino was so shy, Lawrence was their undisputed leader. One day a friend took them by car to Mitla, an ancient Zapotec burial site 33 miles away. Mitla's central chamber walls were covered with repetitive geometric patterns, like hoofbeats in stone. One of Brett's photos shows the Lawrences intently examining the high stone walls.

Lawrence always intended to rewrite *Quetzalcoatl*, the novel that both he and Frieda prized, and so he worked quietly in the garden during the winter. It was likely that Frieda influenced many revisions that Lawrence introduced as he recast the novel, now called *The Plumed Serpent*. In part, her increasingly assertive behavior roused him – in reaction – to make the main female character, Kate Leslie, more eagerly responsive; and to make the admired males, Cipriano and Ramón, more masculine, dominant and godlike. Of course, such revisions reflected both Lawrence's clearer understanding of his characters and his waning strength. But something festered inside him. He feared that his malaria, the dark fruit of Ceylon, had returned. Feeling out of sorts, he confessed to William Hawk in January that he had "wondered why I wasn't well down here".

Lawrence improved his novel in many ways – for example, in the fine poetry that gives solemnity to the Quetzalcoatl religion. But as he patiently rewrote, Frieda finally acted on her jealousy of Brett's camaraderie with Lawrence. Never intimidated by Frieda, Brett could be arrogant and even mocking. At last Lawrence, though hating domestic "scenes", especially when he wasn't well, asked Rosalino to deliver a letter to Brett: "You should [now] go your own way," he insisted. Unwilling to agitate Lawrence or to battle against Frieda, Brett agreed to return to Del Monte and, in the high winds and drifting snow above Taos, occupy the Danes' cabin. Miserable but undefeated, she left Oaxaca on 19 January. Frieda had won this skirmish.

But in another sense she hadn't. Lawrence's revised novel, pocked with irritation, reveals his emotional crisis. Kate is radically reshaped to become yielding and submissive – less like Frieda, more like Brett. Turning 40 (as Lawrence would soon do), Kate crosses the line from trust to bitterness, from congeniality to loneliness, from health to worry. She is easily discouraged. Much around her – the bullfight, the peasants, the dirt, the lice – disgusts her. Only strong men awaken her. To charm them, she shows not her penetrating intelligence but her "soft repose" and her "mystery." Craving completion, she begs the gods "to put the magic back into her life, and to save her". The "magic" is not love but a force found in religion and embodied in Ramón. More powerfully than in *Quetzalcoatl,* he intuits that Mexico needs an indigenous spiritual revival. In this man's presence Kate feels dazzled,

>─┤◆├─○─┤◆├─<

honoured to serve, and grateful that, as a married man, he's unavailable for sex. That was Brett's position exactly. Kate is ennobled but not entangled by Ramón's religious fervour.

Lawrence took a big risk in reshaping Kate. Mesmerized by men and their religious enterprise, she lacks the brilliance or complexity of Lawrence's earlier heroines. Exhausted in spirit, she yields her body not to Ramón but to his lieutenant, Cipriano. She becomes now "just a woman", her core gone soft. In sex, the show is his, his climax. He wants her to gush "noiseless and with urgent softness from the volcanic deeps". He teaches her the erotic power of passivity: but by then she has become a black-and-white photo of her old, discriminating, *Quetzalcoatl* self. Sadly, with Cipriano, Kate will enjoy "no personal or spiritual intimacy whatever". She settles for so little that it's hard to see how Frieda thought Lawrence's new work "a great novel", because it is so profoundly marked by systemic illness. His publishers, when they read it, knew it would not be popular; later, even Lawrence agreed.

He had been working so feverishly on the novel that by January Frieda found him "exhausted". The novel had grown "like an enormous cactus", she observed. But when he came to the end, his intestines erupted. He had been hit with influenza or typhoid, and was soon dehydrated. Brett having been sent away, Frieda valiantly nursed him herself. But in February he got worse and couldn't stand up. The Mexican doctor whom Frieda summoned failed her. In a recently published letter, she wrote, "The Mexican doctor *simply* did not come, from laziness or from fear of being responsible; so all fell on my shoulders. I did what I could and [now] have pulled him through." She moved Lawrence back to the Hotel Francia, where the Americans living in Oaxaca could help. For ten days he lay helpless, at the edge of death. He and Frieda hated Mexico. "I never wanted to be here," she told her mother, "but [Lawrence] was as if bewitched by his Mexico."

CHAPTER 15

In late February Lawrence, full of quinine doses, and Frieda, battling fierce depression, boarded the slow, rattling train for Mexico City. They stayed a month at the expensive Hotel Imperial. Lawrence got thinner and thinner. His X-rays were ominous. His doctor told Frieda that her husband was unfit for the long sea voyage to England, uttering the dreaded words "Mr Lawrence has tuberculosis." It was a sentence of death. Although Frieda shrugged off the hateful verdict, she agreed to take him back to the Kiowa Ranch, where, despite the brutal cold, he might recover. It took all his courage – and all Frieda's energy – to climb aboard the train for El Paso, where, when the doctor at the border heard Lawrence cough, the authorities would not admit him into the United States. Frieda made a scene. They were, she complained, "tortured by immigration officials". When the American embassy in Mexico eventually intervened, the Lawrences fled north from El Paso. In Santa Fe, Frieda did not take him to a nursing home to recover, though Witter Bynner was nearby and indoor plumbing available. The expense deterred them. Thomas Seltzer's regular payments had stopped. Feeling poor again, Lawrence would need to publish a lucrative novel: he must have wondered whether the elaborate rituals of *The Plumed Serpent* went too far. Once at Del Monte, the Lawrences were almost home. Brett and the Hawks, Rachel and Bill, graciously provided for them.

But Lawrence's illness was a turning-point. He was never the same after Oaxaca – weaker than ever before. That he might write still another novel seemed unlikely. No longer a disciplined writer staring down illness, he had become a fragile, frightened man who, every day, pleaded with the gods to give him strength. "The only gods are men," Ramón had finally understood. The message they offered was part of Lawrence's slow recovery. The gods that Lawrence had been looking for in Mexico, emerging from his own heart, told him that love might be expressed not in passion but in calm acceptance and that loyalty might include betrayal.

For now, the big risk was the collapse of his health. In early April Lawrence and Frieda moved the two miles up to Kiowa, where Trinidad Archuleta and his wife Rufina came to build fires and carry water. The ranch's isolation and pristine beauty were miraculously soothing. Home at last, Lawrence spent every hour trying to get well. "It made him deeply, almost religiously happy to feel better again," Frieda wrote.

Chapter 16

The Road to Spotorno

➤━◆➤━◦━◅◆━┥◄

Lawrence had always liked taking risks. But this time Death had issued him a solemn warning. At the ranch above Taos, he lay quietly on the narrow porch that Brett had helped him build. While Frieda cooked and cleaned, and helped keep him calm, he slept for hours and hours. The healing sun seeped into him like a potion. Indoors he watched the blowing snow. "Really," he had cried, "one ought to be able to get a fresh start." A fresh start was less likely now. By his own account he was "half awake". Both Lawrence and Frieda longed for change: Frieda for some of Kate's magic to come back into her life, now freshly burdened; Lawrence to return to a place, even if he only imagined it, where he had been well.

As a couple they had different but equally complex journeys to make. Very early Lawrence knew that his journey to recovery would take him back into his past – to England and the Midlands, then south to Italy and the Mediterranean. He would move from the arid mountains to the sea, and from a challenging Mexican novel to a series of short pieces. Frieda's journey, though in one sense parallel to Lawrence's, would diverge in startling ways.

At the ranch the Lawrences' orbit contracted. They rarely went to Taos, and were rarely visited. Lawrence, still ghostly pale, believed he would regain his health by simply resting, for, as Frieda lamented, people "make him tired, because he pours himself out to them". Remaining below, at Del Monte,

➤━◆➤━◦━◅◆━┥◄

Brett often rode up – sometimes for tea – and brought the post. She soothed Lawrence as no one else did. However, her sketch of Frieda at the ranch that summer is mainly hostile – Frieda appears rough, rude and temperamental, ordering Lawrence about, dismissing first Rufina and then Trinidad, Lawrence powerless to stop her. Half in jest, Brett once threatened to "rope her to a tree and hit her on the nose". Though Frieda liked the busy ranch, she was also discontented, having uneasily "reclaimed" Lawrence in Oaxaca, where she had written angrily to her rival, Brett, "You know I wish you well, but my life is my own and I don't want you to boss either my life or my ranch – And you would soon do both as your will is stronger than mine." Frieda was still the *wife*, able to play the marriage card whenever she felt threatened. Whereas Lawrence preferred a triangle with Brett, who validated him, Frieda felt diminished by it and fought for her power and status.

The hard work at the ranch required the Lawrences to hire strong men to help them. Scott Murray, who charged them $50, constructed an irrigation system so that the ranch, usually parched, would have water. Before departing, Trinidad, turned part-time coachman, hitched the horses Aaron and Ambrose to a new buggy and, while singing softly, would drive the Lawrences away for an afternoon. Fred Alires, a young Mexican from San Cristobal, came and sweated for two dollars a day. In May arrived Frieda's nephew, Friedel Jaffe, Else's 21-year-old son, who had been studying in America. He was tall, dark and agreeable. Living in Brett's tiny cabin, he helped with all the chores. Frieda acquired chickens, and Lawrence a cow named Susan; he milked her every morning at 6 o'clock and every evening after tea. The Lawrences now had milk, butter and eggs – and also a small garden. They were becoming self-sufficient.

Lawrence, he wrote, "never felt less literary". Unwilling to deplete his remaining strength, he wrote only a few dozen letters the whole summer. Any effort carried a risk.

However, for a Santa Fe friend named Ida Rauh, an actress with masses of curly hair, he began to work on a biblical play he called *David*. When Ida listened to Lawrence read through the whole play and sing its songs, she responded with cool appreciation. At 48, she felt too old to play the young Michal. She did not, however, dampen Lawrence's or Frieda's enthusiasm. The play, dotted with archaic language, captures Lawrence's moving away from evil spirits and death, as embodied in King Saul, towards the simple beauty of the love between David, soon to be King of Israel, and Michal, Saul's lively daughter. David's ascension to power mirrors the growth of their love. Frieda liked the play so much that she translated it into German. Though never published, her translation celebrated Lawrence's return to health.

If *David* is one exploration of power, another lay at the tip of a rifle. Lawrence, increasingly concerned with power relations, saw how – even at the ranch – he could make fresh sense of a death he had caused in August. In "Reflections on the Death of a Porcupine", one of several essays he wrote that summer, he meditates on an animal he had shot with Brett's .22 rifle. At the ranch, killing rats, chickens, chipmunks and, at times, porcupines (because they gnawed the tops of pine trees) was necessary. But it stirred Lawrence to reflect on the natural hierarchy of creatures and their compensatory capacity to attain heaven (what he calls the Fourth Dimension). That the strong will vanquish the weak was already familiar. But in rethinking this idea, Lawrence argues that inequality has a purpose rarely acknowledged – to provide every creature with a meaning beyond itself. Every living thing, he says, while striving to become more than itself, "quivers with strange passion to kindle a new gleam, never yet beheld". The key word is *passion*. Long ago Lawrence had found passion in the body. Now he abstracts it from the body and endows it with a spiritual dimension. Having in Oaxaca come so close to death, Lawrence redefines Christian ideas of everlasting life: sacrifice is no longer ennobling; nor is equality. What ennobles is the ability to embrace *hierarchy* on the route to fulfilment. Fullness of being replaces good works or reverent meditation. Lawrence's turning-point is, however, temporary. It lasts only until his waning sexual feeling forces upon him, by 1926, a renewed appreciation of the body.

As Lawrence contends with power relations and their effects on the soul, the curve of his writing begins to follow the curve of his marriage. Over his career he had modulated from passionate love stories to marriage conflicted, soured or doomed, to a fascination with a spiritualized landscape – as in the porcupine essay. The perennial favourite of all Lawrence's short stories, however, bends backward, along the curve of a child's toy ... a rocking horse. As the story opens, a marriage lies in crisis; its familial love has collapsed into cold duty. A failed father, depleted of worth, complements a materialistic mother whose selfishness she cannot hide. Their young son Paul silently pleads for love. He is in crisis too.

This story, "The Rocking Horse Winner", came to Lawrence ten days before he gave up the ranch in September 1925, although he delayed drafting it for several months. A journalist named Kyle Crichton had sought Lawrence's advice on portraying a young boy. "You've got to use the artist's faculty of making the sub-conscious conscious," Lawrence advised him. Look beneath the boy's "unending materialism", he added, to find "the hidden stuff". In "The Rocking Horse Winner" Lawrence does. He returns to his painful Eastwood past to portray a boy obsessed with pleasing his mother. For Lawrence it was a bewildering topic, since "the hidden stuff" would require him to see himself in Paul's desperate bid to win his mother's love. For inspiration – and insight – Paul begins rocking a nameless wooden horse. All the while the walls of his family home mock him (as the subconscious becomes conscious) and whisper, ever more urgently, "There *must* be more money! [...] There *must* be more money!" The maddened walls stir

><><><-0-><><-<

Paul to ride harder and harder, in a masturbatory fantasy that leaves him exhausted – but also knowing who will win horse races like the Derby. Through an agent, Paul bets money and wins – more and more money. Like the eponymous Woman Who Rode Away, Paul rides after new knowledge, finds it, even invests on the strength of it – then discovers its cost: "he fell with a crash to the ground". Though unconscious, he utters the name of the Derby's winner before he dies in the night. The boy's unselfish attempts at love, defeated by the materialism of his culture, are rebuffed by harsh, insurmountable barriers to fulfilment. The boy leaves life believing he was lucky.

For Lawrence, however, leaving the ranch in September really meant turning his back on life in America. Living at the ranch was too hard, despite its gift of fierce independence; the daily round was too taxing; he didn't thrive. Frieda, feisty about seeing her children in London, had fuelled his irritation. He was, Brett reported, exhausted by his "incessant feeling of hostility". His courage remained, but he wanted to shed his awful irritation. Arriving in New York City, the Lawrences saw well-to-do people like Alfred and Blanche Knopf, now Lawrence's American publishers, as well as friends like Nina Witt, who lent them her apartment in Washington Square. Frieda had lunch with the Seltzers but found them horrid and condescending, apprehensive about their business which was on the point of collapse. Their many attempts to become solvent had failed.

As usual, the Lawrences' summer visits delayed their decision about where to settle for the winter. In London during September, they spent a weekend with Martin Secker, Lawrence's firmly committed publisher, who, along with Knopf, gave Lawrence a comfortable advance on *The Plumed Serpent,* now in production. In America, Lawrence's account at the Chase National Bank of New York showed a balance of $1,002 on 30 September; six months later it stood at $2,254. Lawrence had been paid well enough to think that in Italy he could afford a house on the Mediterranean. At last Frieda saw her children in London, although she openly complained to Brett of jealousy: "I rejoiced in the children, but alas, they are jealous of L[awrence] and L[awrence] jealous of them, can you believe it? And I between." However, whereas William Gerhardie, a new acquaintance, also complained – of Lawrence's "girlish, hysterical voice" and of his flippant judgements – Catherine Carswell found her good friend looking "pinched and small" beneath his wide-brimmed Mexican hat yet bearing towards her family the same kind concern as always. The two dreary weeks that Lawrence then spent in the Midlands, motoring to see his boyhood haunts, depressed him.

The Lawrences escaped eagerly to Germany for two more weeks, where in November they celebrated Anna von Richthofen's 74th birthday. Frieda had her hair bobbed, to make a splash on the Italian Riviera. She was fortifying herself, staking a claim to a little more freedom than she'd had at the ranch. As before, the Lawrences still pined for Italy, and in November followed Martin Secker and his wife Rina to Spotorno, a coastal village 40 miles from Genoa, with a slow, appealing, indolent life.

The Lawrences' journeys around three continents were ending: Frieda would not leave Europe again during Lawrence's lifetime. For Lawrence it was a journey back home, not only to the Midlands but also back home to Italy, the country he loved more than any other. But if he had known what lay ahead, he might never have chosen Spotorno. Within weeks of their arrival, Frieda – now distant from the ranch and the horses she loved – was already reporting to Brett soon after they arrived in Spotorno, "I feel happy – for no reason." As Lawrence soon realized, there *was* a reason.

Chapter 17

Compassion and Rage

❦

I talian sunshine ... for Lawrence it was a pleasure beyond most. Wearing the new suit that Eddie Clarke, Ada's husband, had made for him in his tailor shop, Lawrence arrived in Italy on 15 November 1926. Unlike Frieda, who had enjoyed visiting her three children, Lawrence gladly left behind both the oppressive dampness of the Midlands, where he had "coughed like the devil", and the icy cold of Switzerland, where he and Frieda, coming from Germany, had stopped to visit a friend. They went straight to Spotorno, a little village on the frayed edges of the Riviera, which Martin Secker, Lawrence's gentle publisher, had recommended. The Villa Bernarda, the four-storey house the Lawrences located, sat high above the village and overlooked the blue Mediterranean. The sea sparkled as always in the sunshine. "It's Italy, the same forever," Lawrence told Blanche Knopf, "whether it's Mussolini or Octavian Augustus." In the Bernarda's huge garden, the last leaves were dropping from the grapevines. Behind it rose hills where the Lawrences could stroll when the wind wasn't bitter. Frieda was soon preparing hearty lunches: "I must go [now] and cook some rice and artichokes and fish," she wrote to Lawrence's sister, Emily; the second course included "Gorgonzola and figs and nuts and pears". By 8 December Frieda was chortling to Brett about someone she had met at the Bernarda. This man, coming like an erotic tsunami, swept Frieda away from the safety of her marriage.

❦

His name was Angelo Ravagli (see Illustration 13). He was a peasant from a large farming family where a rough frugality was a way of life. Stocky and genial, two inches shorter than Lawrence, he was a handsome, robust man of 34 who had risen from poverty into the ranks of the Italian Bersaglieri (they were riflemen), where he was now a lieutenant. He managed the Villa Bernarda for his wife, Serafina, who had inherited it, and was helping her bring up their two young children, Magda and Stefano, in the nearby town of Savona. She was a high-school teacher who had acquiesced to her husband's dalliances. Stefano remembered his father as a man who *knew* he attracted women. Frieda described the "thrill" of seeing his dress uniform, and was charmed by him. Open and assertive, virile and expansive, guided by the raw edge of his emotions, Ravagli resembled Otto Gross, who, back in 1907, had similarly beguiled Frieda. Both Gross and Ravagli were seducers.

Soon Lawrence was wary. Frieda had never hidden her emotions – she allowed others to cultivate restraint – but she was surely careful. As Christmas approached, she would not have seen much of Ravagli because her younger daughter Barbara had come to the Bernarda to visit and required her mother's attention. Now 21, Barbara "went for walks and swept and set the table", Frieda wrote, "and in the evenings we drew and sang". Lawrence, too, was enchanted with Barbara. But, for sure, as he sat outdoors on the terrace, bundled in a new overcoat and scarf, he was watching and wondering. The beginnings of a novel were already taking shape.

Beside the Mediterranean, Lawrence, while keeping one eye on Frieda, also blessed the glorious sun, which glittered all day over the water below, and wrote short stories which were typed by Brett, now staying on Capri near the Brewsters. But his suspicions about Frieda's newly discovered romantic interest explain his subsequent behaviour as little else can. For instance, one evening the topic of love elicited an outburst. Frieda, giddy at being reunited with Barbara, had annoyed

Lawrence. Already uneasy about Ravagli's weekend visits to Frieda, Lawrence suddenly challenged Barbara: "Don't you imagine your mother loves you," he hurled at her. "She doesn't love anybody." Then the crowning insult: "Look at her false face." Where, Frieda must have wondered, was his love? Had it gone?

February brought more tumult to the Bernarda. Lawrence's sister Ada came for a two-week visit, bringing a friend. Frieda's daughter Elsa arrived, also with a friend. Add Barbara – and that made five strong women and one weakened man; and on 5 February he was hit with what, though he called it the flu, was a bronchial haemorrhage – "worse", he told Brett, than at the ranch in August. It's not clear whether a doctor came, but Frieda and Ada collided over how to nurse Lawrence. He could no longer mediate.

Hurt by Ada's insults (Ada locked Lawrence's door), yet determined to enjoy the company of her beautiful daughters, Frieda jumped ship and went with them to a nearby hotel. She had tired of the abuse. Lawrence, still feeble – and still miffed – rose from his sick-bed and left the Bernarda with Ada and her friend. They went to Monte Carlo as the two friends headed toward England. "I'm so awfully sorry there was that bust-up to spoil your holiday," he told Ada a few days later. "I had so wanted you to have a nice time." The fragile threads connecting husband and wife had come apart.

Alone now, where would Lawrence go? He seemed, Barbara said later, "really shattered". In times of acute distress, he always went south. Suddenly he bolted. On 26 February he sent Brett a telegram. He had written her such entertaining letters, and so many, that she had formed an illusion or two of her own. His telegram read "VENGO A CAPRI" (I'm coming to Capri). She was astounded.

After a jubilant reunion with Brett and the Brewsters, Lawrence, despite looking wan and collapsed, put his maleness to a test. It was a profound mistake. As February ended, Lawrence surely believed that he and Frieda had separated again – though this time Frieda's girls were, he may have guessed, a diversion from Ravagli's persistent affections. Lawrence fretted that he was "tired to death" of the Bernarda's friction. During the 1923 separation, Lawrence had found no one but Götzsche to share his nomadic life; but on Capri he found the Brewsters, the adoring Brett and others. Feeling now a warm sense of accord, he spent many happy days on the narrow beach at Piccola Marina and at the Brewsters' villa – although one evening he complained bitterly about Frieda's disloyalty to him: "Women are hardly ever true to themselves" and consequently "they are not true to others". He minded her disloyalty, not because she felt entitled to sexual fulfilment but because he could not see the shape of his own future, and therefore couldn't decide where to go. He hated having so little money for travel when he wanted to hire a yacht and "go away for a time". He had illusions of his own.

Nevertheless, on 14 March he and Brett went off by themselves to the mainland to visit Ravello, a picturesque town high up over the Mediterranean, where they took adjoining rooms in the Hotel Palumbo. Having spent hours roaming Ravello's narrow streets, setting up their easels to copy statuary at the stately Villa Cimbrone, hiking in the hills behind the town, talking and resting under the shade trees, Lawrence and Brett naturally drew close. He was glad for companionship without friction, she for the opportunity to cover him in the glow of her love. Their time together was like a honeymoon without the life ahead.

Then one night, after saying goodnight, Lawrence went into Brett's adjoining hotel room, got into her bed, offered a kiss and made tentative sexual overtures. Inexperienced, she responded as best she could; but Lawrence could not sustain his overtures and, feeling disappointed and diminished, abruptly left her room. The next night he visited again, more confident of the outcome: "I felt desperate," Brett recalled. "All the love I had for him, all the closeness to him spiritually, the passionate desire to give what I felt I should be giving, was frustrated by fear and not knowing what to do. I tried to be warm and loving and female. He was, I think, struggling to be successfully male. It was hopeless." But whether suffering from dysfunction or fearing failure, Lawrence endured a brutal blow to his ego and, blaming Brett, fled to his room. He was humiliated, and though Brett was as kind and forbearing as always, he was relieved when she went to Naples to check on her immigration status. She wanted to go to America with Lawrence. He never saw her again.

He didn't want to. When Brett wrote to him, probably to declare her passion and her misery, and to beg him to meet her somewhere, he lashed out in anger: "The greatest virtue in life is real courage, that knows how to face facts and live beyond them. Don't be Murryish, pitying yourself and caving in. It's despicable. [...] Rouse up and make a decent thing of your days, no matter what's happened." In one sense he'd had his revenge on Frieda without, in this instance, being unfaithful. In another sense he had freed himself from imagining a future with Brett. It was, he understood, Frieda or nothing. That was a painful truth. Yet Lawrence knew that, despite the intense struggle with her, he loved her as he had loved no other woman. In such a mollified frame of mind, confident that his bond with Frieda had strengthened, he meandered by way of Florence back to the Villa Bernarda, where Frieda had raised a white flag.

He was welcomed with joy. Luckily, Frieda's daughters, still at her side, had assumed Lawrence's role as antagonist and sparring partner. On 11 April he wrote to Earl Brewster, "I find Frieda very much softened. [...] Finding her own daughters so very much more brutal and uncompromising with her than I am, she seems to [have changed] her mind about a good many matters." Still, for Frieda the ground on which to resurrect their love – and their marriage – had become unstable. To herself she would have admitted that the strength of her love had declined, while her sense of loyalty to a famous man, who enhanced her standing as no other man had, checked her tendency to "lay the law down". A departure from Spotorno might put them on higher ground.

On 20 April they gave up the Bernarda and went to Florence; they both loved the city, and Frieda wanted her girls to see the jewel of Europe. Florence also had the special advantage of not being near Savona. Early in May, from the Lawrences' base at the Pensione Lucchesi, they heard from a new friend, Arthur Wilkinson, a bearded puppeteer, about a 16th-century villa outside the city. It was called the Villa Mirenda. When they saw it, the Lawrences were entranced. It was larger, more impressive and more nobly situated than any house they had ever rented. They took a year's lease – then extended it to two. On 3 May Lawrence wrote, "It is quite lovely in its way" – a big, heavy villa (see Illustration 9), perched on a hill, with two gardens and, nearby, three peasant families to work the land. Frieda liked it too: "My heart went out to it. I wanted that villa." The house, almost unchanged, still stands today. In 2001 Alessandro Mirenda, gazing out from the high windows of the villa he owns, observed, "Questo è il panorama che i Lawrence potevano ammirare; si estendeva per molte miglia." ("This is the view the Lawrences had; they could see for many miles.") Below the windows, neat rows of grapevines fell away from the knoll on which the house sat, slipping down past the olive trees to the gentle stream below; and near this stream, after the summer heat had passed, Lawrence sat, his back to a tree, to begin the novel that was to make him famous the world over. In it appears a gamekeeper who, though he owes much to Lawrence and the English Midlands, has some of Ravagli's sexual appetite. The titled lady at the centre is as unfulfilled – and as hungry

– as Frieda. The novel became *Lady Chatterley's Lover*. It is Lawrence's and Frieda's story, cunningly disguised. Out of it comes the most eloquent portrait of disloyalty ever written. It is full of compassion, rage and profound disappointment.

Chapter 18
Exposing Their Secret

>−◄►−○−◄►−◄

In the Italian spring the Lawrences watched the peasants at work in the vineyards and happily anticipated the ancient grape harvest in September called *vendemmia*. They had seen the big open vat in the basement of the Mirenda, where barefoot men would take turns treading the ripe grapes. While Lawrence waited for the torrid summer drowse to pass – too hot to start a new novel – he and Frieda travelled across northern Europe. There they escaped the Italian heat. What they could not escape were their marriage's broken boundaries. In the flow of unpublished letters that Frieda wrote to her mother, there is an odd two-year gap (1926–1927). After Frieda had met Angelo Ravagli, her letters home may have been too candid for preservation and destroyed. A reference in a later letter (*c.* 28 April 1928) suggests that her mother, Anna von Richthofen, knew all about Ravagli. Excited by his passion, Frieda had welcomed Ravagli's romantic overtures. Tired of nursing Lawrence, she did not believe that wifely duty was a sacrifice worth making: "that's not what I understand by life", she later insisted. In 1926 the Lawrences' intimate feelings probably went unexpressed. They had rebuilt their marriage on a smaller foundation.

While the strands of their feeling came together again, the Lawrences spent their early days at the Mirenda painting shutters, buying furniture and cookware in Florence, whitewashing the walls and carpeting the living room. They carried picnics down to the stream, admired

>−◄►−○−◄►−◄

the willow trees (which Lawrence later painted in vivid reds), picked the wild yellow tulips and, as the nightingales sang, walked in the soft pine woods nearby. They loved these joyful times together. To their neighbours Frieda, boisterous with laughter, described Lawrence at the Taos ranch chasing his cow, scolding her and shaking his finger in her face. The Lawrences' deep companionship had become a compensatory source of strength.

Together they went to Germany to celebrate Frieda's mother's grand 75th birthday, then to England for Lawrence's family reunion, which was complicated by the recent ugly feud at the Bernarda. That feud left Lawrence going alone to Scotland, to see a friend; to the English coast to see his two sisters, who for now avoided Frieda; and then to a bungalow he had rented at Sutton-on-Sea, Lincolnshire – where Frieda, joining him, could swim vigorously in the surf. Surprisingly, the visit empowered rather than oppressed Lawrence. He liked being "back in my native Midlands", he told his old friend Koteliansky. In long conversations, his sisters had denounced the horrors of England's coal strike – called to protest against the miners' wages and working hours – and the damage it was inflicting on Midlands families. In the aftermath Lawrence began to sympathize with the common people – the very people, after all, from whom he had sprung. That was important. In his rich creative imagination two strands of material were joining. The theme of adultery, recently so familiar and disturbing, and the theme of England's conflict between miners and mine-owners, now so much on his mind, were coming together in a story different from any he had told before. He needed Italy's quiet, placid days to write it.

Arriving in early October, for the last of the *vendemmia*, the Lawrences relaxed in the Mirenda's cool interiors. They savoured the peace of the old villa and delighted to find masses of sweet, newly harvested grapes. "It is very lovely [here], really – not like autumn, like summer," Lawrence wrote. Then a change. The man whose response to the coal crisis had intensified to a maddening pitch ("I am always thinking about the strike," he said) could no longer contain his bitterness. On Saturday 23 October 1926, he picked up his cushion, notebook and fountain pen and went into the pine woods to write.

The proof of what was on his mind comes from his English neighbours, Arthur and Lily Wilkinson, radical expatriates who kept a diary and who invited the Lawrences to tea. When the guests arrived on 24 October they were ready to quarrel:

> The talk soon got on to Revolution and stayed there and was really impassioned. We all generalised a bit – but [Lawrence] did so tremendously and swears by his class, and death and damnation to the other class. He's done with them.
>
> "They're hard – cruel, cruel" (crescendo). He was so rude and cross to [Frieda], and she retaliated with spirit:
>
> "Why didn't you marry one of your own class then?" she said. "You'd have been bored stiff."
>
> Says he, very sad and vinegary: "I may have my regrets."
>
> And she retorted: "Well, you can be off – you can go *now* if you like."
>
> It was rather tense – but we got them off that tack and, though the talk on their part was so savage, we daresay it did them good to let off steam.

Two things seem surprising – how easily Lawrence could still get worked up, and how his generalizations could still cause Frieda (who could have ignored them) to retort. A week later Mrs Wilkinson acknowledged that Frieda "speaks up for herself boldly". Lawrence of course resented her quarrelsomeness, even though he provoked it. The prim Wilkinsons, despite always wanting to "change the subject", reveal that class conflict had wormed its way into the Lawrences' marriage and formed a wedge. Did Lawrence "damn" those with power? Did he have "regrets" about his marriage? In his new novel, he could explore class divisions, the arrogance of mine-owners, and the limits that love and sacrifice could impose on a wife. If Frieda was "bold" in her speech, so was Lawrence – and he was about to expose the secret between them.

Lady Chatterley's Lover came out of Lawrence's powerful imagination in three parts (1926, 1927, and 1928), each surprisingly different. Each justifies adultery, but each increasingly understands the cost of crossing class boundaries (as Lawrence and Frieda had done) to find fulfilment. Lawrence's early novels had been explorations of extreme feeling; his middle novels, adventures into other cultures; *Lady Chatterley's Lover*, the most explicit, discovers with increasing precision the stages of sexual bonding. The first version, written in just four weeks, cracks open the Lawrences' secret with the least guile. It dissects in rapid episodes a conventional, upper-middle-class marriage rooted in compatibility and entitlement. Beneath the couple's assumed happiness, they share a profound hurt. The defining fact about Clifford Chatterley is his impotence. It is the key that unlocks the story, because, although he has had every advantage – education, land, an inherited baronetcy – he lacks the one potent power that would hold his wife. He is D. H. Lawrence in disguise.

Connie Chatterley, however, now 25, refuses to be a victim of her marriage vows. Educated like Frieda partly in Germany, she has come to love her husband as Frieda loved Lawrence: "She loved him in her peculiar, neutral way." The couple are lovers no more but "true companions". Clifford acknowledges that Connie has always felt "a heavy, craving physical desire", and he agrees to her having a lover "if you have to!". Connie's needs are uncomfortably close to Frieda's. Many more such parallels make Lawrence's story the most provocative he had written.

In time Connie moves toward rescue, even as she shocks herself and others by taking as her lover a lowly gamekeeper named Parkin. A brown-eyed Ravagli of the woods, he also has served in the army, carries a gun slung over his shoulder, does not speak proper English (it is an irony that in Spotorno, Lawrence had tried to improve Ravagli's English) and fights the coal strike by becoming a Communist. He too has been hurt by a big, florid, insolent wife – named Bertha – who, like Frieda, has "gone loose while he was away". All three characters – Clifford, Connie and Parkin – suffer, yet crave relief. Clifford has the life of the mind – books, literate conversation, painting. That leaves Connie and Parkin, disillusioned and lonely, for whom only one experience can awaken them. That is sex, Lawrence's forte. In a pivotal scene Parkin arouses Connie to ecstasy:

> For the first time in her life, passion came to life in her. Suddenly, in the deeps of her body wonderful rippling thrills broke out where before there had been nothingness; and rousing strange, like peals of bells ringing of themselves in her body, more and more rapturously, the new clamour filled her up, and she heard and did not hear her own short wild cries as the rolling of the magnificent thrills grew more and more tremendous, then suddenly started to ebb away in a richness like the after-humming of great bells.

Although the novel's later versions will introduce Connie to the rich vocabulary of the senses, in this first stage of her education, she must learn the elements of passion. At once, she begins to cleanse impurities from her mind: class bias, patronage, philosophical abstractions, élitism rooted in privilege. Yet Connie and Parkin rarely talk; Lawrence speaks for them. He gives Connie's body a voice, a stream of beautifully articulated feelings. "Passion has dignity," he had declared. Indeed, he gives their bodies *a sacred voice* that commands respect. For readers that was new. Connie and Parkin try to preserve the religious awe they feel within themselves. Their future hinges on their ability to sustain their sacred connection. Though the novel ends hopefully, it does not propose a future between them. Lawrence could not hand the unfaithful woman a ticket to happiness. For him that was still too painful to contemplate.

Having quickly completed the first version, Lawrence welcomed the mild autumn at the Mirenda and saw a few friends whom he especially liked. One was Giuseppe "Pino" Orioli, at the centre of Florence's gay enclave – a rotund bookseller, hugely entertaining, and as excited by scandal as his bawdy companion, Norman Douglas. Once *Lady Chatterley's Lover* changed direction, Orioli would make himself famous as Lawrence's private publisher. Other friends came too. Driving up to the Mirenda in a new car (an Itala) were a couple Lawrence had known for years – Aldous and Maria Huxley (see Illustration 10). Aldous was tall (6 feet, 4 inches), a Cambridge graduate who (like Lawrence) had been a schoolteacher. He was now a writer of distinction, having published 15 books, including *Crome Yellow* and *Antic Hay*. Maria, his petite Belgian wife who had been Lady Ottoline's protégée during the war, had a special liking for Lawrence. The Huxleys, living on an income that Lawrence envied, had travelled the world. They also provided intimate portraits for the novel's second version.

Mostly, Frieda confirmed, she and Lawrence lived quietly at the Mirenda. Christmas 1926 brought the local peasants to see the Lawrences' tree, decorated with shiny ornaments. After handing out wooden toys to all the children, the Lawrences enticed the girls to sing, then served cakes, candies and dessert wines. They loved such festivities. A month later the Wilkinsons observed that, after all had partaken of tea and Lawrence's hot potato-cake, "Mrs Lawrence was in great form and just went for the piano in the most relentless way, and sang as well as played the accompaniments." Perhaps afterwards she smoked one of the cigarettes the Wilkinsons had given her for Christmas. Later, she stayed busy sewing jackets, dresses and a coat for herself. She would look splendid in her new wardrobe, Lawrence told her mother.

All the while, Lawrence was working steadily on the second version of the novel. He finished it in February. This time he wrote slowly, exploring the "bottomless pools" of his imagination. In this version, nearly twice as long as the first, Lawrence makes the love story far more persuasive. He introduces Cambridge intellectuals like Huxley who aridly debate the concept of immortality and therefore neatly motivate Connie's escape into the woods of Clifford's estate. Lawrence also begins to lift the gamekeeper out of the working class. He makes him an anomaly – a sensitive, suffering man who has gone back to his Midlands roots because he refuses to "get on" in the world; he becomes more like Lawrence – though his "medium build" and "military erectness" resemble Ravagli's. But Lawrence's rage, now intensified, feeds new diatribes from a narrator who castigates money, class hatred, power and gossip: "Our society is insane," he rails, his tone gone shrill.

In the second version the sexual scenes, much expanded, are shaped into stages of developing sensual exploration, from intimacy to religious revelation, from daytime encounters to night-time experiments. When Connie sees the keeper's naked torso, for instance, she feels "she had touched God". As important, Lawrence adds a night of sensual passion with a surprising anal dimension. Still ... Lawrence, though he carefully revised the manuscript, decided not to publish it. Once he realized that with Orioli's help he could issue it privately, right there in Florence, he knew he could print whatever he wanted and avoid the strictures of publishers like Secker or Knopf. He would write the whole novel again, even though the effort would be immense. He would compromise nothing, neither full frontal sexuality nor brutal indictments of Britain. In short, the novel's first version startles readers with its story, the second slaps their faces – the third would punch them with its fist.

But after Lawrence had finished the second version, his health worsened in the damp February weather – his flu, he wrote, "not bad, but beastly". All winter Frieda had delighted in how well Lawrence felt, and the Wilkinsons don't mention a serious illness until 10 May, then call it "malaria". But when the summer heat descended on Florence and sent all living things into a prolonged drowse, Lawrence one July day picked all the ripe peaches in the garden, came inside – then cried out from his bedroom. He could barely speak. Blood gurgled from his mouth. His lungs had haemorrhaged. He and Frieda were terrified.

Chapter 19

The Final Version

>-+-»-0-«-+-<

A few months before his stunning tubercular haemorrhage, Lawrence had taken an "Etruscan" walking trip with Earl Brewster, whose tact and wisdom made him a trusted companion. Like Arthur Wilkinson and Aldous Huxley, Earl had stamina, a little money and a strong marriage built on affection and respect. While Frieda went to Germany for a month, Lawrence journeyed to Ravello to visit the Brewsters. In April 1927 he and Earl set off for ten days to see the Etruscan ruins north of Rome. To earn money he would write travel sketches of the sites where the ancient Etruscans had lived, focusing on the decorated tombs at Cerveteri, Tarquinia, Vulci and Volterra, where, he said, "man moves naked and glowing through the universe". That glowing nakedness gave Lawrence a "phallic shock" similar to what Connie felt on seeing the gamekeeper's body in *Lady Chatterley's Lover*, the novel that still lay in manuscript at the Mirenda. In discovering the Etruscans' physical vitality, Lawrence rediscovered the past, as he had rediscovered the Midlands. But the past was slipping away fast, his mortality ever more evident. Like so much at this juncture in his life, the walking trip was the last of its kind – like the last trip to America, the last novel to be issued by Secker and Knopf, the last glimpse of Brett, the last meeting with Murry, the last evening with Frieda's son Monty. The doors were closing.

In July Frieda, burdened with anxiety, decided to move Lawrence, now very sick, to a cooler climate. His

>-+-»-0-«-+-<

haemorrhage "keeps coming back", he complained. Weak and often exhausted, he mended slowly while Giulia and Pietro, their servants, did all they could so that Frieda could be a full-time nurse. The mustard plaster used in the past provided little relief, and at night, Frieda reported, he dripped with sweat. Dr Giglioli, on his daily visits from Florence, demanded bed rest; Lawrence, though impatient, co-operated. The Wilkinsons found him "so good and patient that one hardly knows him". In the steamy heat of 4 August, they finally got the Lawrences into a hired car and off to the train station, there to catch the night train to Austria.

The cool weather of Villach, the Austrian resort town where they met Frieda's sister Johanna, was a fine tonic. At Irchenhausen, they stopped at Else's wooden chalet, their temporary home in 1913. To treat his advancing tuberculosis, Lawrence drank tumblers of goat's milk. Then, as always, they went to Baden-Baden to visit Frieda's mother. There a doctor found his bronchial tubes inflamed and recommended a ten-day inhalation cure. Daily, for an hour, Lawrence grimly endured the cold steam from radium springs. He also took Junicosan to loosen his phlegm. Nothing helped much. His health in jeopardy, he hoped "to get well as soon as possible". But after so much haemorrhaging, he knew the tissue of his lungs was badly damaged.

His novel, lying dormant since February, would – he knew – be called "pornographic". If he were going to rewrite it, he couldn't delay. On 19 October he and Frieda returned to the Mirenda in time for the *vendemmia*. The Wilkinsons met them; Frieda looked very buxom, Lawrence very sick. Though thrilled to be home, he complained that Italy had "no life in it". He was, the Wilkinsons reported, "very irritable" with Frieda, and she "dreadfully sharp" with him. His keenest pleasure was to impugn the Brewsters, who had spent their capital, saved nothing, then tried to live in style. They lacked frugality, proportion, good sense. Lawrence's irritation left little room for benevolent feelings. In such an agitated state he was about to begin the final version of *Lady Chatterley's Lover*.

Lawrence wrote it in only six weeks, from 26 November 1927 to 8 January 1928. His handwriting, large and loose, forecasts the change. The final version is more rigid and damning in its denunciations, but more sympathetic to Connie and the gamekeeper (he is now called Mellors) and their urgent need to be healed. In short, Lawrence now makes illness more central, widens the class divide, endows Mellors with intellect and introduces a layer of contempt. What makes Lawrence's book famous is not the story of adultery, but his renderings of female sexual experience. What makes it so pungent is his hostility to his failed society. He skirts the smear of pornography by making the book's sexual encounters the source of life, when all around – at Clifford's estate Wragby, in the mining village Tevershall, in society at large – forms of death threaten to extinguish the little flame of connection that binds Connie to Mellors.

Above all, the new novel prizes tenderness and compassion. Now the opening chapters show how insensitive are privileged people: Clifford's egotism is more pronounced, and his bullying, especially of his private nurse Mrs Bolton, more subtle. But Lawrence does more. He adds an entirely new character, named Michaelis, who illustrates the kind of cad whom Connie in her loneliness chooses as a lover. The narrator mocks his cheap appeal: "You couldn't go off at the same time as a man, could you?" Michaelis sneers. His attack, at a moment of emotional surrender, devastates her.

Unlike Clifford and Michaelis, Mellors is substantial and intriguing. His experiences reflect those of Lawrence's early life, while his mature views reflect Lawrence's sad, vinegary voice. Having escaped from the working class – and become like Ravagli a lieutenant in the army – Mellors is stronger than the insecure Parkin of the earlier versions. Stiffly controlling his feelings, he is now a man's man – vigorously heterosexual, abusive of authority and self-educated. He is also "quite the gentleman". That was what many observers thought of Lawrence.

Mellors has also transcended the values of every class, subjecting each class to a scathing critique. Achsah Brewster reports Lawrence's saying that he didn't belong "to any class of society". No class guaranteed integrity of being. Even Lawrence rethinks the prejudices of his characters and, for instance, repositions Mrs Bolton's narrative about Bertha Coutts, and gives it to Mellors, who knows at first hand his wife's sexual egotism. Her abusive egotism is like Michaelis's. Hence both Connie and Mellors have been damaged by the same modern "disease". Everywhere the novel mistrusts what any class can offer.

But beyond the boundaries of class, the gamekeeper boldly educates Connie. Now he offers her a far more confident sexuality than any she has known. Lawrence masterfully separates restorative impulses from deathly sensations. Michaelis's orgasm, for instance, is quick and selfish, a form of masturbation, whereas Mellors, sensing that Connie is unsatisfied, pauses briefly, then begins once more "the unspeakable motion [...] swirling deeper and deeper", until she reaches an intensity that, in her unconscious cries, connects her to God. The body is the tiny temple of the universe. The unspeakable motion is the rite of connection. The orgasm, cleansing and purifying, is the resurrection.

Stage by stage, Mellors takes Connie from daylight intercourse to night-time experimentation. He initiates, she responds. But the ultimate scene, of anal intercourse, worried even Lawrence. The words become abstract and indirect as they describe a night when, once she "let him have his way", he "stripped her [...] and made a different woman of her". Even Lawrence, struggling to give passion *dignity*, observed boundaries. Mellors can freely use the word *fuck*, but Lawrence will not describe the sensations of

>―←◆→―0―←◆→―<

anal intercourse, preferring filters like "burning the soul to tinder" or she "thought she was dying".

The many alterations in the novel yield, like a poisoned barb, a new register of contempt that grows out of Lawrence's bitterness and chagrin. Contempt is the currency of people like Lawrence who have abandoned love. Michaelis is a "Dublin mongrel", Clifford is "like an idiot", and Connie's sister Hilda labels men "nasty, selfish little horrors". This is the language of insult and attack. It is not that Lawrence has lost his direction, but that his angry need to reform society is so intense that it sometimes obscures the novel's underlying compassion. That was the risk he ran in writing the novel while he was ill.

By protecting the lovers from the hard shell of social decay, Lawrence faced a new difficulty – bringing them into the future. At the novel's end Connie, now pregnant, goes to her sister in Scotland, Mellors to a farm. With her inheritance Connie may buy him a farm – she hasn't yet – so that he can work. (He has only a small pension.) But Connie has rejected an upper-middle-class system without yet knowing how to replace it. Lawrence, despite his great courage, *wasn't sure* if an unhappy person should leave a marriage in order to find love, or should honour loyalty and remain married. *Lady Chatterley's Lover* has it both ways: though Connie leaves Wragby, Clifford, contented on his estate, enjoys his own sexual stimulation – kissing Mrs Bolton's breasts. Yet this fantasy raises the question of which behaviour is moral. If one considers only Connie's fulfilment, she was right to go. But if she and Mellors do not live together – they may not – then Connie's fulfilment is temporary. Still, Mellors's final letter to Connie illustrates his persistent courage: "We fucked a flame into being," he concludes. All boundaries then fall away from the deepest inner connection between a man and a woman. It links humanity to the cosmos.

In its final version the novel stands surprisingly close to Lawrence's life. The married woman leaves her sick husband, as Frieda considered doing. The sick husband finds an alternative form of sexuality, as Lawrence attempted with Brett (managing, like Clifford, just some kisses). The gamekeeper, evolving from the militaristic Parkin/Ravagli to the brave Mellors/Lawrence, allows Lawrence to explore both sides of his personal dilemma. The novel's sex scenes were so shocking, the contemptuous tone so unfamiliar, that Lawrence long disguised his and Frieda's life story of 1926 and 1927; but he openly struggled with the claims of love and loyalty. In 1923 he told Thomas Seltzer that loyalty came "far before" love, but *Lady Chatterley's Lover* argues that love is as important. Love *and* loyalty are the two pillars that braced Lawrence's life. They would become the pillars of Frieda's later claim for his greatness.

But the demands now placed on a professional writer like Lawrence were complicated. He had to produce a typescript, design the book, correct proofs – and groom Pino Orioli (see Illustration 11) to be his private publisher. The six months that followed – from the novel's completion in January 1928 to its publication in June – were among the most stimulating and rewarding of Lawrence's short life. Each step towards publication led him into new territory of risk. He had already invested in the speculative American stock market – on 8 September he had sent a cheque for $4,000 to Bonbright & Co., an investment firm in New York; now he needed to invest money in a novel whose sexual content would preclude copyright protection. Worse, he had no professional experience in design, production, marketing or distribution. For a man as sick as Lawrence – at Christmas, Frieda thought him "very weak" – he took amazing risks. "I am determined to [publish] it," he told Orioli.

Lawrence had good reason to finish the manuscript quickly. He and Frieda had accepted the Huxleys' invitation to Les Diablerets, Switzerland, for a winter holiday from 19 January to 7 March 1928. In the snowy Alps, Lawrence, staying mostly indoors, arranged to get his novel typed. Catherine Carswell

><><-0-<><><

and her friends helped, as did Maria Huxley, who typed the last half. By 5 March he happily possessed a corrected typescript in triplicate: one copy for a printer in Florence, one for Secker in London, and another for Knopf in New York. (Against all hope he had lightly expurgated the "commercial" copies for Secker and Knopf.)

Then, despite his good spirits, came a sudden dose of unshielded anger. In March, the Wilkinsons met the Lawrences at the train station in Florence, listened to their venomous tales about the Huxleys and watched the Mirenda's peasants toss spring flowers into their car, and then, one week later, heard Lawrence say – apparently in Frieda's hearing – that if he were making a will, he would insist on a clause: "Not a penny if [Frieda] marries again! Not a penny!" If Lawrence made a will with such a provision, excluding Angelo Ravagli from touching his assets, it did not survive. A month later Frieda had her covert revenge. Disliking her role of nurse and martyr to Lawrence, she admitted to her mother that "with every bit of inward strength, I make myself slowly freer". Like Connie to the keeper, she had been writing to Ravagli.

For Lawrence, however, other matters were more urgent. On 9 March he and Orioli met in Florence, then carried the typescript to the old-fashioned print shop, the Tipografia Giuntina, where the typesetters worked by hand. If they had spoken English, they might have perused the 423 pages of *Lady Chatterley's Lover* and been surprised. The real shock came a few months later, when the United States Customs blocked the book's entry into America, and British booksellers cancelled their orders. "Damn the Americans – damn and damn them," Lawrence wrote in panic.

Chapter 20
Where to Go?

⊳·◄▸·○·◂▸·◅

In all this excitement around the publishing of *Lady Chatterley's Lover* Frieda seldom participated. In her unpublished letters she rarely mentions Lawrence's work on the novel. She cooked lunch of pigeon and broad beans, went for long walks with Lawrence to see the violets and red tulips, prepared tea, modelled an arm or a leg when Lawrence (as a break from writing) began to work at large oil paintings, went shopping with her servant Giulia, and in the evenings sewed or embroidered. The Tuscan spring made her, she said, feel "blissfully happy". She supported Lawrence in his grand publishing experiment, but they had grown far enough apart for her not to read his proofs, fetch them from Florence or help him with business letters. The publishing thrill was his. Even he barely understood the splash he would make outside mainstream publishing.

Rushed into action, Lawrence needed a strategy. The various authorities he had hoped to flout as long ago as 1915, when they had attacked *The Rainbow*, had not disappeared. But now, backed by his own money, he could distribute *Lady Chatterley* as he wished, outside commercial publishers, and circumvent the authorities. Still, he admitted, the novel will "set me apart even more definitely than I am already". The typesetters in Florence quickly printed 1,500 order forms that Lawrence could distribute to his friends, and 600 that Pino Orioli could send to booksellers. The novel's price was £2 or $10 for a signed and numbered copy (roughly £75

⊳·◄▸·○·◂▸·◅

or $150 today). By 1 April Orioli – who had agreed to a commission of ten per cent of the novel's proceeds – brought Lawrence the first proofs; they revealed a chicken-pox of error. Frieda later remembered the book's "thousands and thousands of mistakes". Worse, the Giuntina, a small outfit, had only enough type to set half the novel. The workmen had to stop and print 1,000 copies on handmade paper and 200 on cheap stock (later sold as a second edition), then "set" the novel's second half in May and June. But the challenge inspired Lawrence. "It's rather fun doing it," he told Koteliansky. Because Lawrence was so famous, orders flooded in – 500 from England alone. He knew he could sell his Florence edition.

In June he felt confident enough in Orioli's supervision to leave the Mirenda for the Swiss Alps, where he hoped the cool air might help his lungs "make a cure". Coming for a visit, the Brewsters, when they saw Lawrence dressed so neatly in white flannels and blue coat, yet looking so pale and thin, suddenly realized, Achsah wrote, "that he was very ill". They quickly agreed to join the Lawrences on their journey north. It was the kind of venture they all liked: singing hymns in the train, exploring the quaint shops, reading the long menus in French. But at a rustic inn, the hotel manager knocked at Earl Brewster's door: Lawrence had been coughing all night, a local law banned tuberculars, they must leave. Eventually the Lawrences went higher, to Gsteig-bei-Gstaad in Switzerland, at 4,000 feet, where Lawrence gasped going uphill but still rented a little cottage in the mountains. The amiable Brewsters stayed below in a hotel, coming every day to tea. Lawrence thought he was better; drank Ovaltine and other concoctions; invited his sister Emily and her daughter Margaret, now 19, to visit; then, when the leaves turned in October, went to visit Frieda's mother in Baden-Baden. There he went to outdoor concerts and played cards.

The fun had already begun in July. All summer Orioli sent news about *Lady Chatterley's Lover*. From Florence he posted 200 copies to England in June, while Lawrence, though fluttering with anxiety, offered a guiding hand. "I think you might," he advised, "send three or four copies every day to America" – eventually Orioli sent about 200 – and then copies to English people who won't "talk". Lawrence didn't hear from America until August. Working closely with Orioli – always by post – he wrote batches of letters about the novel and also kept immaculate records of the book's costs, receipts and payments, and names of purchasers.

Despite his precautions, problems quickly arose. Although Orioli confirmed that copies to England "have been delivered without any trouble", London booksellers such as William Jackson and Stevens & Brown, having perused the novel for themselves, began to refuse the copies – more than 100 – that had been delivered to them by post. "Damn them all," Lawrence cursed. He asked his London friends Koteliansky and Enid Hilton to rescue the books and deliver them individually to buyers – or hide them and keep mum. Alas, the United States Customs soon confiscated most copies sent to America. "I shall send no more to America," Lawrence declared. Now he worried that pirates would pounce on his novel and launch their own editions, paying him nothing. The risk increased after 1 September, when Herbert J. Seligmann, an admirer, published a review in the *New York Sun* calling the novel "magnificent beyond praise".

Meanwhile, Lawrence fought for his health. Whereas the Mirenda's dampness had made him feel awful, he imagined that the Swiss mountains would "harden" his lungs. They didn't. After a while he felt worse. His "tormenting cough" never let up. Desperate, he and Frieda decided to try the sea. They accepted an invitation from old London friends named Richard Aldington and Arabella Yorke, who had distributed copies of *Lady Chatterley's Lover* from their country cottage in England. Joined by Aldington's long-time friend Brigit Patmore, the group spent a month on the private French island of Port-Cros. Aldington thought Lawrence's wit now full of bitter malice, but Brigit found it highly entertaining. Lawrence would imitate Earl Brewster's singing, or tell a story about a Ceylonese servant who slithered up behind Achsah and whispered, "If spider bite *lady*, lady die," terrifying her. Lawrence loved to make his listeners laugh.

By this time no one pretended to ignore Lawrence's decline. Even during afternoon swimming expeditions, he couldn't be left alone. Alarmed, Richard would listen all night to "his dreadful hollow cough". As bad, Aldington began paying nightly visits to both Arabella and Brigit, infuriating Lawrence, who had tolerated disloyalty in his own emotional triangle. Worse, Frieda caught the flu in Italy and gave it to Lawrence, who spent two days haemorrhaging. "I should like it here," he told Koteliansky with cruel modesty, "if I had shaken off this cold." When he was better, he lashed out – not at Frieda but at the press clippings that arrived by mail boat. One called his novel "the foulest book in English literature". Infuriated, throwing branch after branch onto the fire around which his island friends had gathered, Lawrence seemed mesmerized by the towering flames. In symbolic disgust he incinerated his enemies.

Failing, Lawrence didn't know where to go or what to do. Every cure had eluded him. He had tried mountains, sea, working hard (at the Mirenda), hardly working, being with people, being alone. All provided temporary improvement, followed by a relapse. Frieda accommodated his indecision, partly because she did not herself know what to do, and partly because she was courting a romantic option beyond her marriage. The little journeys she took by herself – to Alassio, Baden-Baden, Florence – often allowed her to rendezvous with Ravagli. Her stamina and sunny disposition always prevailed.

After facing the rigours of Port-Cros for a month, Lawrence needed a gentler, more hospitable place where his friends, new and old, could also stay. A hotel seemed best. Surprisingly, he had turned his wheel away from the place

>–·–◆–○–◆–·–◄

he had loved the most. "I do *not* want to stay in Italy this winter," he announced. He doesn't explain that Italy was the place Frieda preferred. In the sunny village of Bandol, ten miles from Toulon, they found the Hotel Beau Rivage, small, comfortable and inexpensive, whose owner, Madame Douillet, impressed them. Here they spent the winter of 1928–29. At last they had money. Although Lawrence never got over his early poverty, and still scrimped, he sent money to his sisters for trips, frequently bought gifts, and paid for visitors' meals. On 29 March 1929 he reckoned his profits from *Lady Chatterley's Lover* at £1,240 (roughly $6,200), which, at the Beau Rivage, could have supported him and Frieda for six years.

His declining energy now dictated not only where he lived but what he wrote. For London newspapers such as the *Evening News,* he had discovered that he could – in a couple of hours – toss off short articles on contemporary mores. The best of these is "Insouciance", a gallant plea for us to live not with abstractions like Bolshevism and Fascism but "through our instincts and our intuitions". They connect us to what is best in life – the glassiness of a lake, the sulkiness of a mountain, the sweaty perfume of haymakers. He also tossed off flat, barbed lyrics he called pansies and nettles, one of which ("What does she want?") shows an impotent, frightened narrator resisting aggressive women:

What does she want, volcanic Venus, as she goes fuming
    round?
What does she want?
She says she wants a lover, but don't you believe her.

...

How are we going to appease her, maiden and mother now
    a volcano of rage?
I tell you, the penis won't do it.
She bites him in the neck and passes on.

In a chatty tone, as if talking to a young visitor, he reproves sexually powerful women who, rejecting satisfaction, move from lover to lover. In the last line the bitten object is ambiguous: a bitten *lover* is less disturbing than a bitten *penis:* the latter would suggest Lawrence's fear of castration by a defiant woman. Gone is the manly capacity to offer sexual satisfaction; its failure might bring death. Either way, these skunky late poetic blossoms yield a flavour all their own. Lawrence explores the caverns of his chagrin and discovers there not insight but spite.

The winter days passed slowly. What helped were the friends – a succession of them – who came to the Beau Rivage. They stimulated and entertained the Lawrences. Some came to collect the fruit, now overripe, of Lawrence's experience. The young men were like the sons Lawrence had never had ... counterparts of Frieda's children.

Rhys Davies, a quiet young novelist whose grandfather had been a miner, came in November and found the Lawrences amiable and direct, she generous and laughing, he subtly malicious. After a three-course lunch at the hotel, Lawrence – usually too tired to walk – spent the day lazily watching the bay from his hotel balcony or sitting by the water, recounting for Davies the events of his childhood. In the evening they congregated in Frieda's room for more talk. Frieda curbed Lawrence's barbed tongue. He would criticize her for her excesses – too many cakes, cigarettes, false assumptions – and earn a quick, stinging rebuke. Their differences harmonized into a counterpoint of bright and bitter feelings, but revealed less coherence now.

P. R. Stephensen, a tall, athletic Australian, an Oxford graduate, also came to Bandol. Lawrence admired his "fearlessness". Hoping to publish unconventional books, Stephensen wanted Lawrence to authorize his limited, unexpurgated edition of the oil paintings – 24 in all, mostly of nude men and women – that Lawrence had completed during the *Lady Chatterley* years. Persuaded,

Lawrence wrote a vigorous essay to introduce and defend his "shocking" paintings. As in "Insouciance", he admires those who – like Cézanne – can capture not just the apple but the "appleyness" of the fruit, by seeing it from the front *and* from all around. That was what Lawrence had tried to do in his paintings – to combine intuition, instinct and mind. "My beliefs I test on my body," he said, "on my intuitional consciousness." Stephensen, printing Lawrence's insightful defence of his work, rapidly sold his edition of 550 copies. Lawrence earned £500.

Brewster Ghiselin, a handsome American studying at Oxford, came to Bandol for his winter holiday. In January he and Lawrence discussed beaches, ranches, the working class, poetry; perused the local market in the church square; watched the fishermen; and occasionally strolled together in the pine woods above Bandol. "He rarely preferred to be alone," Ghiselin observed, but created around him an easy, lively atmosphere in which others could appreciate, without condescension, his amusing tales of human absurdity.

Like others who came, these young men enlivened the Lawrences' conversation, roused their spirits, buffered their irritations. They elicited Frieda's irresistible laughter, buoyancy and favourite anecdotes about her husband.

Months before the Lawrences were ready to leave Bandol, however, Lawrence heard that pirates had launched two photographed editions of *Lady Chatterley's Lover*, and asked the Huxleys to verify the rumour. Writing from Paris on 11 December 1928, Maria described a signed copy of the novel she had seen in a bookshop in rue de Castiglione: "but the dirtiest to come – [the price was] 5,000 frs!!" Enraged and forced now to confront the sobering truth about the pirated copies, Lawrence felt too sick to take strong, decisive action. Although he realized in December that he "must really try" to publish a cheap edition, he waited till March 1929 to make his move.

>―◆>―○―◆>―◆

Chapter 21
Masses of Mimosa

>─┤◆├─○─┤◆├─<

"What a game life is!" Lawrence wrote in December, aware of the risks that every move required. To see life as a game allowed him to dodge the warnings about his health, to foil Frieda's fervent desire to live in Italy, and to outwit the pirates sneaking editions of *Lady Chatterley's Lover* onto the market. The game was not yet so much with death as with the fires still smouldering inside him, burning rapidly. "I have to struggle so hard to keep [true to] what I am," he wrote to P. R. Stephensen. Though sometimes suffocating in despair, Lawrence would not yield the game without a final fight.

While Frieda went to Germany, Lawrence went to tend one of the fires. He arrived in Paris on 11 March 1929, accompanied by his quiet young friend Rhys Davies. Before leaving Bandol, Lawrence had bought a new grey suit, shirt, shoes, gloves and hat. He would make a dashing figure in Paris. For a month he and Davies stayed at the Hotel de Versailles, where they were soon joined by Frieda. To save Lawrence from having to brave the strong March winds, she organized grand picnics in her hotel room. Venturing out, she brought back French wine, vegetable salads, cheese, apples and batons of bread – all of which she served as a feast. She skilfully accommodated any need.

On many days Lawrence had too little energy to secure a publisher for an edition of his novel cheap enough to beat the pirates, but finally he and Davies located Edward W.

>─┤◆├─○─┤◆├─<

Titus, a middle-aged bookseller who edited *This Quarter*. He agreed to supervise a Paris edition, and Lawrence wrote a foreword, which became "A Propos of *Lady Chatterley's Lover*", defending his novel as a "healthy" book that aimed to harmonize mind with body. Titus printed 3,000 copies of the novel, to be sold at 60 francs each – as opposed to the 5,000 francs a bookseller had quoted Maria Huxley. Titus reprinted the novel many times, selling copies all over Europe. Lawrence shrewdly demanded half the profits, and before a year had passed Titus had paid him more than 40,000 francs. Still, although Lawrence had fulfilled his goal, the noise and dirt of Paris sickened him: "These big cities take away my real will to live," he lamented. He needed the Mediterranean.

In time *Lady Chatterley's Lover* proved far more popular than Lawrence had anticipated. Apart from the cheap Paris edition, he realized he could prepare a thoroughly expurgated copy for a public edition to be sold in England and America – although he declared, "I'm of two minds about it." Could he, he wondered, "trim the book" into a different shape? As late as July he thought he would "try once more". But Edward Titus, for one, strongly opposed the idea on aesthetic grounds and thought it "a great débâcle of principle to expurgate". Before long, Lawrence's bookseller friend Charles Lahr, working with Stephensen as editor, hired a printer named Graves to produce a Third Edition in his London basement, reset from Lawrence's own Florence edition. Though he approved it in spirit, by the time the secret Third Edition was published Lawrence was dead. However, only an expurgated edition, published without risk of prosecution, could secure for him the book's copyright. That did not happen until 1932, when Secker issued an expurgated edition ten per cent shorter than the original.

Moving from France to Spain (avoiding of course Italy), Lawrence spent two months on the balmy Spanish island of Mallorca, 120 miles from Barcelona, and stayed in the Hotel

Príncipe Alfonso while he waited for the London show of his paintings. At the elegant Warren Gallery, Dorothy Warren, whom he had met years earlier, publicly opened her show of 25 Lawrence paintings, mostly oils, on 4 July 1929. People came by the thousand, stirred by newspaper reports. Although Lawrence imagined that Dorothy would be "afraid of the police", neither of them expected the raid that followed the next afternoon, when inspectors removed 13 of Lawrence's paintings – all those with pubic hair – and charged the Warren Gallery with obscenity. The paintings were sequestered for several months, at risk of being destroyed. Lawrence relished the assault on London's bourgeois viewers, but he hated the threatened destruction of his creative work. He wrote to Dorothy, "No, at all costs or any cost, I don't want my pictures burnt." Some of his smouldering fight was cooling: he stopped painting for good. But the seized pictures were ultimately saved.

Lots of things now upset Lawrence – obscenity laws, pirates, impudent women, illness, doctors. In Germany again, for the summer of 1929, he did allow specialists in Munich to examine him. It was too late for medicine to help. Anyway, he was his own best doctor. He was always getting stronger, feeling a little better, hardening himself.

But the odds in his game were rapidly lengthening. Now a shell of himself, he could hardly walk without pausing for breath. "He is so, so frail!" Frieda told Dorothy. Earlier, Aldous Huxley had noticed how, sapped of energy, "he just sits and does nothing". Yet that autumn Lawrence managed to write *Apocalypse*, the book that eloquently resurrects a pagan vision of the world to help readers escape their fragmentation and become part of a vibrant cosmos whose centre is the sun.

In September, when he returned to Bandol on the Mediterranean coast, he rested one week at the Beau Rivage and then, because Frieda insisted on a house, rented the modern, three-bedroom Villa Beau Soleil, with big balcony windows. He and Frieda remained for four months, till he got much worse. "I lost a lot of strength in Germany," he told Frieda's sister, Else, and with it went his cheerfulness about himself and others. A fresh malevolence infected him: he spoke of his friends with raw spite. Frieda commiserated as best she could and, as she told his sister Emily in December, "I try to be cheerful." The past, too, troubled him. One day he said to Frieda, "Why, oh why, did we quarrel so much?" Typically, she offered no sugared tablet but replied, "Such as we were, violent creatures, how could we help it?" No blame, no apology, no insight – just a calm acceptance of human nature. With the onset of winter, she realized she could do little to help him. Lawrence had to return to the elements, to the stars and sea and flowers, in his own way. The final journey was his.

At last, Lawrence listened to British specialists such as Dr Andrew Morland, who urged him to go to the French sanatorium at Vence to get well. The rest, the good food, the sanitary precautions – all would help. "I am perfectly sure," his close friend Koteliansky urged, "that if you followed Dr Morland's advice you would get well in a very short time." On 6 February 1930 Lawrence yielded and prepared to enter the Ad Astra Sanatorium. He put all his papers in order – destroying many in the process. He decided against making a will. Two months earlier Frieda, acknowledging that Lawrence was "*very* frail nowadays", had written to Brett in the blunt mode she sometimes adopted, "What's between him and me is *there*, if he and I have other relationships, it's all to the good." That is a blithe dismissal of a serious fracture in the Lawrences' relationship: Lawrence felt far more chagrin at her disloyalty than she allowed. His pride rebelled against being churlish and confessing his hurt. Guessing how Frieda felt, however, Lawrence made no provision for settling his Estate. The fight he had waged in his writings was the only fight that mattered. His money and possessions didn't much matter, or he would have given

Aldous or Maria – the most responsible of his close friends – instructions about his will. He couldn't have fathomed the ensuing complications for his heirs.

At the Ad Astra, Lawrence had a pleasing view of mimosa in bloom. The doctors ordered X-rays and gave him injections, but as he said to Maria, "Of course they can do nothing for me." He lost his appetite and could barely walk. Though he felt miserable, he told his sisters not to travel to Vence. Frieda visited him each day and plainly saw the unexpressed horror in his eyes.

Death is – of all opponents – the most daunting. In a sense Lawrence beat even Death. His courage never failed him as slowly he lapsed into "the womb of silence in the living night". Abruptly, on 1 March, Frieda took him away from the sanatorium. He wanted to die "at home". And so he endured a painful, jolting taxi ride to the Villa Robermond which Frieda had rented nearby. The next day, as the end approached, he bravely relied on others. Aldous efficiently made the arrangements, Maria held Lawrence in her arms, Frieda read to him, Barbara cooked. Soon, Lawrence's pain was so great that he pleaded for morphine. A doctor came and administered it. Lawrence, saying he felt better, grew calm, and at 10.30 that night, when his breathing faded like a boat gliding out of sight, he died peacefully, his face a mask of courage. Frieda had never seen him so completely himself. Two days later his body, now in an oak coffin chosen by Frieda, was driven to the cemetery on the hill above Vence. Apart from Frieda, Barbara and the Huxleys, Robert Nichols and Edward Titus – as well as Achsah Brewster and Ida Rauh – joined them. Lawrence's family could not arrive in time. After the mourners, without a ceremony, had quietly said goodbye to Lawrence, they put mimosa – masses of mimosa – on his coffin, covering it before the long shovels of dirt slowly filled in the grave.

Shortly after he died, Frieda recalled how exalted she felt after his final fight had ended:

His death was so splendid [*she told his magazine agent*], so bravely he fought right to the last, he knew quite well about himself, and then he asked for morphine, I think he knew it was the end, then he lay down and said: "I am better now" and soon breathed his last, slow breaths – Dead, he looked fulfilled and splendid, all the suffering gone – I am so full of admiration for his unconquerable spirit that my grief has no bitterness or misery in it – He has left me all his love and all his love for the world – I see him only now as a whole in his simple greatness.

What Lawrence left behind was his lasting gift to Frieda: "all his love and all his love for the world". Misunderstood and maligned, his encompassing love needed, she knew, to be secured for the future. The world must appreciate the purity and the brilliance of his search for a particular kind of manhood, one showing both strength and vulnerability. Even if he left her no will, she felt confident that he had given her the inner loyalty that would sustain her always, and the love that would help inspire her to build a shrine to him in New Mexico. She had lived with Lawrence for so long that she knew what he expected without his having supplied instruction. There were dozens of unpublished manuscripts that, by default, he had entrusted to her. She faced now immense responsibility – and also a mission. To E. M. Forster she wrote that Lawrence "gives me his strength and his love for life".

But now she would require someone to help her. She had not yet learned to be professional and efficient. Her daughter Barbara, though often at her side, was too unstable to assist her. Frieda would have to turn to someone she could trust, someone who was disciplined and unsentimental, someone who might help her honour Lawrence in the years ahead. This person would have to leave behind both a career and a family. Would he do it?

Chapter 22
Without a Will

>━┼━◆━०━◆━┼━<

Lawrence's life – and now his death – meant everything to Frieda. "Dead or alive he is the realest thing to me," she wrote six weeks after the funeral. Yet she had little time to rest. To adorn his hillside grave above Vence, she ordered a pebble-mosaic of a phoenix; she discussed with Aldous Huxley the publication of Lawrence's many letters; in Florence she prodded Pino Orioli to publish Lawrence's *Apocalypse* and beautiful *Last Poems*. But in her letters she sadly acknowledged that Lawrence had made no will. Writing to Edward Titus in April, she summarized the situation if no will survived: "1000 £s for me, pictures [and] Mss mine, but copyrights after my death go to the [Lawrence] family – but during my lifetime *all* the interest is mine." For a while that seemed satisfactory. Why, after a time, did she change her mind? Confronted with a crisis, she thought that without money she could not serve Lawrence, and so she let her hatred of one man direct her course of action.

The fact that Lawrence had made all financial decisions complicated Frieda's life. Lacking his sure hand, she appeared muddled and disorganized. The Huxleys' friend Robert Nichols described her as "stupid" and "unpractical" at the time of Lawrence's death, yet she never put practicality ahead of spontaneous living, and never let a duty compromise an impulse of charity or goodwill. There she was clear. In this respect she was like Lawrence: she followed her inner lights. "I go entirely by my instinct," she declared. Still, she had made

>━┼━◆━०━◆━┼━<

many financial commitments – Lawrence's last expenses, the cost of her daughter Barbara's medical treatments, and her own anticipated travel in Europe and to America, where she had bravely decided to take Lawrence's remains. Luckily, John Middleton Murry, who had come to Frieda's side after Lawrence's death – partly to sample the arts of a widow's love – remembered that Lawrence had made a will. Whether he was doing Frieda a lovely favour, or whether he honestly remembered, is unclear. It would take two more years – till October 1932 – to settle the problem of Lawrence's estate.

While Frieda weighed her commitments and agonized over the problem of the will, she had a series of emotional shocks: Lawrence's friends, including Mabel Dodge Luhan and Dorothy Brett, began to compose their memoirs of him. Brett criticized Frieda (as she always did), while Mabel wrote a full memoir called *Lorenzo in Taos* which portrayed the Lawrences as perversely quarrelsome. Appalled, Frieda realized how these two women had lost Lawrence's essence. Swiftly, impulsively, she froze her own memories of her husband into a romance of love and loyalty. Searching deep inside, she redefined her marriage to Lawrence as a pure smelting of temperaments, out of which grew a love that enhanced their capacity to be alive, but also a loyalty that gave them the freedom to complete what the other had not provided. The truth – as always – was much more complex. Beset by so much tumult, Frieda could see nothing except the way he "grows bigger and clearer for me". She would live for him. Thus simplified, her vision of Lawrence would give her the compass that she had lost.

That compass pointed to America. She would set out, she wrote, "as if I were a young woman" on the way to "a splendid show". At first, she thought that Barbara would accompany her to Taos, but Barbara suffered a breakdown and in November 1930 went to England to recuperate – on the very day that Frieda went to be with her beloved mother in Germany, who died just as Frieda arrived from France.

They never said goodbye. "Fate is cruel to me this year," Frieda wrote to Edward Titus in December. Now, with setbacks in all directions, she needed someone to sustain her. If she were to build Lawrence a shrine at the ranch, she could live in America for six months at a time (the period a visa allowed). Even at the Ad Astra Sanatorium, Lawrence had wanted to return to the ranch, and now, honouring his wish, she would go and prepare the place for his final burial. But the ranch, offering both emotional security and cheap living, had one disadvantage: it was too lonely and remote for a lone widowed woman. She would require a companion.

Frieda had not forgotten Angelo Ravagli. Now a captain in the Italian Bersaglieri, he had met her, on and off, for almost five years, providing what Lawrence could not. Transferred to Pieve di Teco in April, he was at last stationed near his home in Savona. But the pull of his family was not strong enough to hold him. His son Stefano, interviewed in 1998, said that after Lawrence's death, "Frieda was in great trouble. She was very disorganized, and she needed someone who could help her manage the Lawrence estate." The opportunity of seeing America, the challenge of assisting with Lawrence's affairs, and the thrill of obliging a woman flush with money – all swayed Ravagli. Frieda would have to give him a monthly allowance for his help and pay his wife the monthly army cheque she had always received. These were new costs to nibble at the profits of Lawrence's writing. Frieda's relationship with Ravagli, however, was always far more than a business arrangement. His status – he was more than a gigolo but less than a husband – made him insecure, without any moral authority. He put on airs to boost the respect he lacked.

In May 1931, when Frieda and Ravagli stepped off the S. S. *Conte Grande* in New York City, they went to the Prince George Hotel, ambled along the city's streets, and in time met up with Lawrence's American agents and with the lawyer Benjamin Stern, who was helping Frieda to buy back copyrights to

Lawrence's early works. But the Depression plagued America. Many fortunes had plummeted. Maria Cristina Chambers, one of Lawrence's friends, wrote from New York in March, "Four of my dearest friends have [recently] killed themselves." It was not a time to be without money. Boarding a train, Frieda and Ravagli travelled west to Taos, arriving on 2 June. They were now a couple, full of bravado.

Almost at once, they bought Tony Luhan's deluxe La Salle for $800 and hurried up to the Kiowa Ranch, which Brett had made ready for them. There Frieda could inaugurate the simple life again, start a garden and bring back the animals. Yet Brett, loyal only to Lawrence, blared out her contempt of Frieda and Ravagli to all who would listen. In her own romance of the past, Lawrence had, by force of character, poured his chastity into Frieda and stabilized her. Brett, upstaged by the happy new couple, even believed that she was "more truly [Lawrence's] widow than Frieda". She resented Frieda's power to resurrect herself. Confused by all that was happening and especially by her own emotions, Frieda believed that Ravagli "makes me forget my life with Lawrence, that life of otherness". It was not that she lacked reverence for her earlier life but that, in order to live vitally, she had outgrown her need for the framework of marriage.

Mabel Luhan, more worldly and accepting than Brett, embraced the new couple. Invited in July to a grand celebration at the ranch, Mabel found Frieda wildly happy with the tables of food, the strings of lights on a Venetian theme, the music. Couples danced to gramophone music on the freshly raked lawn. "Angelino," Mabel wrote, "is a marvelous dancer – moving tenderly and gravely through the most subtle patterns of the modern step. There is something of the noble child about him and a beauty of cheerful health. We all like him." He was a force, too. In his heart Ravagli was a simple Roman soldier like those who once marched with Caesar. He was physical, practical and full of stamina. He did not deny his appetites, especially for women, and at Frieda's party he reached under the table for Mabel's hand. He was honest and open but also cunning, beguiling, amoral. He was neither analytical nor introspective, nor was he a reader of books. He was a handyman of the highest order. Even Brett, caustic now, acknowledged that Frieda was happier with Ravagli than she had been with Lawrence. "I do like," Frieda acknowledged, "his gentleness and warmth."

At the ranch the summer weeks filled with sudden storms, the arrival of the mail, repairs to the buildings, and visitors who came to see for themselves how the ranch had changed. The La Salle made trips to Taos easy. Yet as the autumn approached, Frieda recognized that she and Ravagli, if they returned, would need to build a bigger, warmer house. She would need money for that, too. "I get into a panic of being without money," she wrote to Philip Morrell. As the walls in Lawrence's story "The Rocking Horse Winner" had whispered, "There *must* be more money."

On 16 November 1931 Frieda and Ravagli, having closed the ranch for the winter, left for New York City. Ravagli had been recalled by the Italian army, and when he returned dutifully to his Bersaglieri regiment he was sent to Imperia, a town in north-western Italy. Frieda shuttled between England, Italy and France – at home in none. She and Ravagli remained in Europe for 18 months, Frieda mostly in London, where she proudly presented herself as Lawrence's widow, capably nurturing his rising reputation. She had lunch or tea with old friends such as Ottoline Morrell, Dorothy Warren, the Brewsters and Koteliansky; she attended rehearsals of Lawrence's play *David* at the Old Vic Theatre; and she visited her three grown-up children. She also met up with Lawrence's young literary agent, Laurence Pollinger, to conduct business. Pollinger efficiently interpreted contracts for Frieda, sought broadcast opportunities and pursued foreign rights, all of which lay beyond her competence. Daunted by these new opportunities, she relied on Pollinger's professional guidance. Especially important was the contract for the 1932 publication of Lawrence's letters, edited by Aldous Huxley and published by Heinemann in London and Viking in New York. This collection of letters presented Lawrence's vibrant immediacy as no other document had. At once Frieda understood its greatness.

She knew, however, that her future depended on how Lawrence's estate would be settled. In 1930 she and George Lawrence, Lawrence's oldest brother, had been named co-administrators – but she detested him, partly because she (and Lawrence) had never trusted him and partly because, as she wrote to Lawrence's sister Ada, "You know how Lawrence would have hated his money to go to George." Lawrence, in fact, had not seen his brother for 15 years. One way for Frieda to honour Lawrence was to guard his money. Unfortunately, her hatred of George and his greed gradually shut her mind to Lawrence's family. Even before the will was settled, a visitor named Emile Delavenay, spending a weekend with Ada in August 1932, recorded "Ada's intense hatred of Frieda".

In time, despite the prospect of a costly lawsuit, Frieda hired an excellent attorney named C. D. Medley to fight George. All compromises soon became impossible. Long before, she had warned Lawrence's sisters that "your brother wanted me to have everything, he told me so, and he and I knew nothing about the law. He thought as I did [...] that everything goes automatically to the wife." It was now time to test her claim in court. After many irritating delays, the judge, Lord Merrivale, heard the case on 3 November 1932. He heard Frieda tearfully describe Lawrence's last wishes, weighed Murry's declaration that Lawrence had made a will in 1914, and pondered the disquieting depositions from Pino Orioli and Norman Douglas that Lawrence had hated his family. Frieda must often have wondered how the judge would lean. When the verdict was read, even she was amazed.

Chapter 23
Manuscripts and Money

Judge Merrivale gave Frieda the whole estate, less £1,000 which went to George and Emily. (Feeling injured, Ada wanted nothing.) Frieda heralded the decision as "a triumph for Lawrence and our life together". At first, she relished the attention that the decision inspired, but she always regretted that her bitter feelings had turned her for ever against Lawrence's whole family. She never saw them again. Instead she went to Savona, to be with Angelo Ravagli and to organize their departure for America. She disliked Europe, which seemed to her close friend Aldous Huxley to have now an "awful sense of invisible [...] hate, envy, anger crawling about". She was eager to tie up all loose threads. "I'm so busy doing a thousand things," she wrote to Knud Merrild, "[that] my life seems full to bursting." Once Frieda had decided to move to America, she set about consolidating her position as Lawrence's widow. In New Mexico she shaped a plan for Lawrence's body, still lying in the cemetery at Vence; hoped to build a new house on her land; and tended her treasure of Lawrence's handwritten manuscripts – at least 175. They were her capital. She hoped that a university might buy them all and keep the collection intact.

Having endured various crises since Lawrence's death, Frieda needed – more than anything – stability. She had weathered the challenges of the will, helped her daughter to recover her health, encouraged the publication of Lawrence's books, bought Ravagli out of the Italian army, and tested the waters of Taos to see whether the inhabitants would permit a widow and a married man to move freely into their midst. Only at the Kiowa Ranch, she recognized, could she be contented with her memories of Lawrence. He had given her the standards that would enable her to live well. "His absolute integrity," she told Mabel, "means everything to me." At the ranch by April 1933, Frieda and Ravagli quickly began to construct a new house a few yards below the cabin that Lawrence had rebuilt. Made of logs, the new house had a big kitchen, a living area, two bedrooms and a bath (and in 1936 a room to hold Lawrence's paintings). Challenged and energized, Ravagli acted as his own contractor and, like Lawrence, hired local labour to reduce costs. In August, Frieda allowed that she had spent only £500 ($2,500) to build the house. While Ravagli laboured, Frieda cooked, gardened, washed clothes, fed the lambs and made butter from the rich milk of her Jersey cow, Anita. In the evenings she sewed and read.

Now she could honour her commitments to Lawrence. Knowing that he would have wanted her to write about their life together, she began working on a memoir. To guide her she had only her memories and some letters, no firm anchor such as the journal that the Arthur Wilkinsons had kept in Florence. But she went forward. Moved to compose lyrical vignettes of their life together, she portrayed Lawrence with a directness and authority that only she could have mustered. The couple's supreme love and undying loyalty figure most prominently. When she had finished the book, she asked Walter Goodwin, owner of the Rydal Press in Santa Fe, to publish it in a fine limited edition of 1,000 signed copies. He issued it in June 1934 as *Not I, But the Wind*. Serving as Frieda's secretary, Ravagli sent out circulars to advertise the book, which sold steadily. In October, the Viking Press in New York published a slightly shorter trade edition, and in England, her friend Alexander Frere-Reeves brought out the British edition for Heinemann. Many admirers wrote her letters.

But as winter approached, Frieda and Ravagli faced a difficulty they could hardly have imagined. Always gregarious and charming, Ravagli had befriended a man named Nicolas Luciani, who with his wife specialized in unscrupulous acts. Luciani had a dream that, with money borrowed from Frieda (a rich widow), he could start a winery. Always generous, Frieda lent him $1,100 – more than she had paid for the La Salle. Suddenly the local sheriff descended on the ranch and accused Ravagli of participating in a scheme (hatched by the Lucianis) to solicit women. Nor was Frieda spared. She was accused of stealing trinkets which Luciani's wife, on a visit, had "planted" in the new log house. Fearing deportation, Ravagli fled. Frieda quickly followed him, driven in her La Salle by the faithful Knud Merrild, who had been visiting for ten days. She met Ravagli in Alamosa, Colorado. They drove to New Orleans and, still fleeing, sailed in December to Buenos Aires, where Ravagli's sister and brother lived in dreary poverty. Frieda and Ravagli did not return to the ranch till spring, when the Lucianis had disappeared to Laredo.

The escapade had given Frieda a warning about Ravagli's caprices but also a fresh appreciation of New Mexico's freedom and landscape – what Lawrence had most loved. In the blazing spring sunshine at the ranch, she and Ravagli planted the vegetable garden, made flower-beds around the house, set out fruit trees, rode the horses. She most enjoyed, she said, "looking after things here at the ranch, like my life with Lawrence was". She had never abandoned Lawrence's spirit. "I have had such a lovely summer here at the ranch," she wrote in August 1934. "People and work and sunshine." In the ten years since 1924, her life had changed little, except that now, well financed, she could memorialize what was most important. That was a shrine for Lawrence's remains and a plan for getting them to America.

She sent Ravagli to Lawrence's grave in Vence, France, on 5 December 1934. Assisted by Frieda's friends, Ravagli was eventually able to get permission to disinter Lawrence's body, take it to Marseille for cremation and, in April, having seen his family in Italy, sail from Villefranche on the *Conte di Savoia* and bring Frieda a box of precious ashes. "I am glad [Lawrence] is no longer at Vence, with all the scandal," she wrote. At last Lawrence might have eternal peace.

But Frieda did not know that Lawrence's Taos admirers were concocting a caper that would hurt her deeply. Mabel Luhan, now more manipulative than ever, gathered a few friends who determined that Lawrence's ashes belonged not to Frieda but to the world. Nothing could have enraged Frieda more than a covert attempt to steal part of her life with Lawrence. When Brett unexpectedly joined forces with Mabel – and, worse, when Frieda's daughter Barbara and her husband Stuart Barr, visitors to the ranch, swelled Mabel's camp of antagonists – Frieda was appalled. She espoused the "standards" of openness and honesty that Lawrence had taught her. She felt viciously betrayed. "I was so shocked and angry," she wrote. At that point, flanked by Ravagli, she made a bold decision: she would mix the ashes with mortar and pour the concoction into the altar of the little chapel that she and Ravagli had built a few months earlier on the hillside above the ranch. There Lawrence would be safe for all time. On 15 September 1935, she organized a grand ceremony around a huge bonfire to consecrate the ashes. Three Indians sang songs. Mabel's entourage did not attend.

Frieda may have foiled her enemies, but she had not reckoned her full costs. The Depression had altered everyone's outlook on money. Books sold more slowly, and in London Martin Secker's publishing business, like Seltzer's in America, had failed. Although Frieda and Ravagli lived cheaply at the ranch by virtue of doing all their own work, the harsh New Mexico winter forced them to journey to Los Angeles, where, although the sun shone splendidly, the high-flying film studios had inflated all costs. Yet Frieda had wisely held back her most prized asset: Lawrence's manuscripts.

There were unique – immaculately handwritten, sometimes without correction. She knew she could sell them. In Los Angeles she met a German woman named Galka Scheyer, who led her to an enterprising young bookseller specializing in manuscripts. His name was Jake Zeitlin. Poor but ambitious, he was thrilled that Frieda should ask him to sell the manuscripts and, when he saw the collection, found it "simply overwhelming". His shop assistant was a brilliant young man in his twenties named Lawrence Clark Powell, who after meeting Frieda and Ravagli on 1 April 1936 immediately recorded his impressions:

> I liked her immensely. We talked a good deal in the shop and then at lunch. Her voice is German and hoarse, her face is weathered, fine. She is alive and hearty and warm-hearted. [...] Her Italian bersaglieri [...] is short, husky, curiously boyish, shy. [*Fifty years later, Powell added:*] He was volatile, genial, a very companionable guy. But I spotted him. He was a wolf, really – a satyr.

Larry Powell believed that Frieda tolerated Ravagli's lust for other women because he made few demands and performed whatever service she required. On the same day in April, Jake was already letting a client peruse Lawrence's manuscript of *The Rainbow*. For prospective buyers Jake commissioned Larry Powell to prepare a descriptive catalogue of all the manuscripts. Before he could do so, Frieda went back to the ranch and welcomed an energetic young couple from Harvard University who stayed with her for ten days. They, too, were fascinated by the manuscripts.

Their names were Harry K. "Dan" Wells and his wife Jenny; today Jenny lives in San Cristobal, a few miles from the Kiowa Ranch. Talented and outgoing, they came from moneyed families, had gone to the best American schools and, in order to gather material for a proposed biography of Lawrence, had spent a whole year, 1935–36, travelling by bicycle all over Europe. They approached those who had been close to Lawrence and, wherever they could, bought his letters and manuscripts, including some from a big trunk that Pino Orioli had stored in Florence. They met Frieda's sister Else, Jessie Chambers, Lawrence's sister Ada and Bertrand Russell.

When Frieda invited the Wellses to the ranch, they were ecstatic. Arriving in August 1936, they found Frieda dressed in a plaid Bavarian costume. She greeted them with gusto and warmth. "It's like being in another world," Jenny wrote. They loved it so much that they bought 40 acres nearby. When Dan Wells discovered how many manuscripts Frieda possessed, he was eager for Harvard University to buy them, so that he could have full access for his biography (never written). To that end he arranged for Jake Zeitlin to ship them to go on display in Harvard's Treasure Room, and for Frieda to give a talk in December on Lawrence's poetry. For two happy months Frieda and Ravagli stayed with the Wellses. Jenny was surprised at how open their relationship had become, Frieda apparently unruffled when Ravagli took other women to dances. "They seemed," Jenny said, "to be able to enjoy each other's company without being possessive."

To persuade Harvard to buy all the manuscripts, Frieda and Jake agreed on a special price. It was $25,000 – about half their appraised value: for Jake urged Frieda to keep the collection together. Amazingly, Harvard declined the offer. Lawrence's work was still too bold, too tainted. The library's director, Robert P. Blake, wrote smugly to Jake that "our rather limited resources" could not accommodate the cost. That single decision would have profound consequences for Lawrence's manuscripts. They would be dispersed – a few lost, many entering private collections long off limits to scholars. In May 1937 Dan Wells returned the Lawrence collection to Jake, for whom Larry Powell – paid $100 – spent the month of June writing a sales catalogue. But in the depths of the Depression, when a loaf a bread or a quart of milk cost only a nickel, there were few buyers.

Though well-off by Taos standards, Frieda was worried. She had bought a new car in 1936, had invited the Huxleys to spend the summer of 1937 on her ranch (where they required a bathroom in the original cabin), and wanted to oblige Ravagli's wish to build a swimming pool. Then came temptation. In October a neighbour offered to sell her his big ranch, four miles from Taos, which would be warmer and more convenient in winter. She wanted to buy it, but worried she couldn't afford it. Then, to her dismay, Jake Zeitlin, fallen low, thought he might be forced into bankruptcy. In time he returned the manuscripts, mostly unsold, to Frieda. It was a low-water mark.

Chapter 24

A Home on the Coast

Distressed, Frieda knew that she would have to reduce her expenses or increase her income. Earlier she had spent $2,000 retrieving the American copyrights of most of Lawrence's books, but in 1938 she arranged for Random House to reprint the Thomas Seltzer titles and to pay her substantial royalties. In an act of serendipity, Jake Zeitlin had introduced Frieda to a rich, eccentric manuscript-collector from Pennsylvania named Thomas Edward Hanley, who began to buy the unique manuscripts of Lawrence's essays, short stories and full-length novels. Eventually he bought at least 60. Hanley became Frieda's golden goose. "It *would* have been a mistake to sell to Harvard," she reminded Jake. Now, if a big expense arose, she gathered an egg from Hanley. And she did what she had done for years – tried to publicize Lawrence and to develop her talent for friendship.

Before Hanley appeared, the Huxleys had arranged to spend the summer with Frieda and Angelo Ravagli. Disillusioned, they had left Europe for ever. Driving across country, they arrived at the ranch on 1 June 1937, Maria at the wheel of her Ford, her passengers Aldous, their son Matthew and a friend named Gerald Heard. All four pitched in to help Ravagli build a bathroom in the Lawrence cabin. Writing to a friend, Maria, glad that Aldous was able to work again, celebrated the unsurpassed views of the desert below and praised Frieda's generous, affectionate nature. But she was amazed at the primitive life that Frieda lived.

Worse, Frieda allowed visitors casual, easy access to her: "Frieda is continually visited out of the blue by vague friends or strangers [who] want to see Mrs D. H. Lawrence." Frieda allowed them access because she was always generous. Maria refused: "I firmly say Aldous is working." A European at heart, Maria found America an alien, unconquerable country; Frieda found it bracing and beautiful. Maria minded all the hard work, the scrubbing and sweeping, that ranch life required; Frieda didn't bother if the work didn't get done. She left it for another day.

But as autumn approached, Frieda was forced to reconsider winters at the ranch. They were brutally cold and snowy, as she knew from the winter of 1922–23 which she and Lawrence had spent at Del Monte. Now that she was approaching 60, the simple life had grown more daunting – roads washed out by storms or blocked by snow, supplies far away, no maid to assist her. She had considered moving off the mountain to the Taos plateau. Suddenly a piece of property was available: Edward von Maltzahn's 300-acre ranch. He and his wife wanted to return to Germany. Partly as an act of friendship, she agreed to the purchase, paying him $4,500 cash in October 1937. His ranch was beautiful, with soft plains in one direction, bold mountains in another and the Indian Pueblo in still another. Near the main road sat a fine adobe house. She called it the lower ranch and stayed there, off and on, for the rest of her life. Ravagli groused because, with two places to manage, he now had twice the work; but he would be able to pursue more easily his new diversion, pottery, which he practised when he visited Italy in the winter of 1937–38. He believed he was an artist too. He wanted to build his own kiln and earn his own money.

But whatever he earned couldn't compare with Ed Hanley's fortune. Hanley had millions. For a group of three manuscripts, including the expurgated typescript of *Lady Chatterley's Lover*, he paid Frieda $1,900 in ten monthly instalments, beginning in January 1938; then $3,000 more in instalments for seven additional manuscripts. Staggering sums they were – more in total than she had paid for the lower ranch. Doling out money in instalments was not, however, Hanley's only eccentricity. Big and square-shouldered, dull and taciturn, he came to Los Angeles each winter, looked at what Jake Zeitlin had for sale, then reserved what he liked until he was ready to buy. "I would have to be patient and listen to him every day," Jake remembered. "He was the world's most God-awful bore." On Saturdays what excited Hanley more than manuscripts was the circus: he knew all the clowns, the acrobats, the showgirls – and he eventually married an Egyptian belly-dancer named Tullah. Yet he had exceptional taste in rare manuscripts and as late as 1956 was still making monthly payments to Frieda.

Very often Mabel Luhan, and sometimes Brett, left Taos for the winter. Frieda was equally tempted and, using Hanley's cheques, went every year from 1937 to 1941 (and occasionally thereafter) to the perfect climate of southern California. Ravagli liked it too. They stayed in apartments costing $100 or so a month. Hollywood gave them more than climate. It gave them access to a set of glamorous new friends whom they met through the Huxleys. When Aldous began working as a screenwriter in Hollywood, he and Maria met directors, writers, actors, even scientists. In 1938, for example, after Ravagli returned from Italy, he drove Frieda to Hollywood for Occidental College's production of *David*, the play that Lawrence had written at the ranch. There they visited the Huxleys and, during this visit and one the following winter, met the Huxleys' friends, among them Grace and Edwin Hubble. He was a gifted astronomer who studied galaxies, she a cultured graduate of Stanford. Meeting Frieda at the Huxleys' apartment, Grace found her handsome and powerful (see Illustration 12),

> like the women Tacitus wrote of who followed their fighting men through the ancient forests of Europe. She was sitting

on the lounge, a broad-shouldered, deep-chested, shapeless bulk in a burgundy-red chiffon dress, and long strings of beads, and grey stockings. [...] Her blue eyes danced or looked straight through one, and she laughed a great deal.

Grace admired Frieda's aristocratic bearing, more serene now but still striking. All noticed how much Frieda laughed; the abrasive intensity of the Lawrence years had faded. Frieda also met Charlie Chaplin and movie star Paulette Goddard. Performing wickedly funny imitations of Hollywood stars, Chaplin delighted his guests; like Frieda, Paulette loved to entertain. Another young writer named Dudley Nichols took Frieda to see director John Ford filming *The Long Voyage Home*. Affable and creative, Nichols became especially close to Frieda. "To me," she wrote, "you are almost a symbol of the best in America." He read Lawrence with special sensitivity, and he admired how she had preserved the ranch. She was naturally appreciative of the kindness and warmth of these new friends.

Frieda also promoted Lawrence. She found a publisher, the *Virginia Quarterly Review*, for two early plays and an unpublished story discovered in London. In Hollywood she approached William Dieterle, a German director, hoping that he would film *The Plumed Serpent* in Mexico, from a script that she and a writer named John Beckett had crafted. In 1940 she sold the film rights to *Lady Chatterley's Lover* and implored Aldous Huxley, Zoë Akins and Christopher Isherwood to work on the script; sadly, these highly-paid writers were too busy. When Isherwood visited Frieda in April 1940, he found her lively and interesting but "already an old woman", hawking "hopelessly undramatic" material. Undeterred by rejection, Frieda marched loyally on. Her enthusiasm for Lawrence's work was contagious, but her ignorance of the rapid technological changes in the film industry hampered her efforts. She had abundant energy but lacked expertise.

><+>·0·<+·<

However, in 1943 in Santa Fe she met a man named Willard Hougland who helped her publish a manuscript she had long held back. He interested the Dial Press in New York not in adaptations of Lawrence's work but in the unpublished first version of *Lady Chatterley's Lover*, which Dial subsequently issued in April 1944. Frieda wrote to Dudley Nichols, "I always loved it best." The original print run of 17,500 copies quickly sold out after a vice squad, headed by John S. Sumner, charged the book with obscenity. His charge, which garnered a lot of free publicity for the book, was overturned that November.

While Frieda occasionally met with success, America's war years of 1941–45 left her and Ravagli in a muddle. A German and an Italian living in a country at war with their native lands, they were always uneasy. Though he often listened to the radio for news, Ravagli tried not to think about the war and his family – and always kept busy. Frieda, however, remembered all too well living in Cornwall the last time England had been at war with Germany. "I am so very sick of war and more war. It makes me so angry," she told Richard Aldington, who had also come to America. He advised her to go quietly about her life. Unfortunately, the British government had blocked royalties and dividends for all expatriates, so she and Ravagli were forced to be more frugal. For the most part, from March 1942 to December 1944 they sequestered themselves at the lower ranch. They contented themselves with meals at Taos restaurants and long visits from friends. By now Frieda was also a chain-smoker, never far from a packet of Camels.

In time, even the lower ranch – despite Ravagli's many improvements – offered winters seldom relieved of the cold wind gusting from the mountains. In Taos Frieda had met an attractive widow named Johnie Griffin (see Illustration 13), originally from Philadelphia, whose Texas oil wells had made her almost as rich as Ed Hanley. She liked Frieda and Ravagli, and offered them the use of her comfortable house near Brownsville, Texas, 1,200 miles from Taos; there they stayed for several months from December 1944. Ravagli (and sometimes Frieda) could fish in the port channel, while Frieda also now had time to herself, flowers to cut from the yard, the scent of orange blossoms, wild quail to watch in the fields nearby, and days of peace to help her forget the war. As she wrote to Dudley Nichols in 1945, "One can only try and hang on to the best in oneself."

Two years later, after one more sojourn in Hollywood, Frieda began to remember the simple life she had spent on the lakes of Italy and on the sparkling Mediterranean. From long afternoon drives around the Gulf of Mexico, she knew that near Brownsville lay secluded hamlets and beaches in the winter sun. In January 1947 she and Ravagli again drove south to Brownsville, on the border with Mexico, and then to a waterfront settlement five miles from Port Isabel, Texas. It seemed, Frieda told Knud Merrild, like a European fishing village, the kind she knew well. There she bought a flat seaside lot with a small house. From its windows she could see the fishermen's boats in the channel, the bright-winged gulls, and the wild ducks forming patterns across the sky. "It keeps on being fun here," she told Brett. The place, though it needed landscaping and lots of repairs, might well prove to be the place of her retirement. With Ravagli, she was settling into comfortable routines. She was 67.

Chapter 25
A Pair in Perspective

◄►—◄►—O—◄►—►◄

These were winters of blue skies and red sunsets. Frieda's move south from the Taos mountains to Port Isabel on the water echoed the moves that she and Lawrence had often made – to Lake Garda in 1912, to Taormina in 1920, to Lake Chapala in 1923 and to Bandol in 1928. In those places they had loved the bright light, the freshness of the walks, the fishermen with their boats and nets. Frieda had always felt "moored" by Lawrence, by her mother and at times by her three children. Now all had changed. She had severed her ties to Lawrence's family; her mother and husband were long dead; and she rarely saw her children. Angelo Ravagli, though he was affectionate and hard-working, had not met many of her emotional needs. To create an alternative, Frieda gathered around her a group of close friends, many of them unmarried, who turned to her as to the sun – for warmth, generosity and understanding. Frieda spent her last years replacing the families she had left in Europe.

These friends and occasionally relatives brought her the homage she still enjoyed as Mrs Lawrence. Near her lower ranch, for example, Frieda had given Brett two acres of land; William Goyen took two acres for a small adobe house; and Willard Johnson enquired about *his* two acres. Frieda soon had a neighbourhood. In January 1947, going south to Port Isabel, Texas, for the winter, Frieda learned that her vibrant younger sister Johanna, penniless after her property in Austria had been confiscated, would visit her in America.

◄►—◄►—O—◄►—►◄

She was jubilant. At the side of the small waterfront house, Ravagli built Johanna a large bedroom full of windows. Lawrence having made possible this reunion, Frieda hoped for others like it.

But some of her relatives could not so easily come to America, not even for a wedding. In Taos, Frieda married Ravagli on Hallowe'en 1950, partly to be sure that he could inherit half of her estate (which he did), and partly to ensure that he could return from Italy without difficulty. When he went again to visit his family, in April 1952, Frieda acknowledged that – for herself – she had the resources to buy a round-trip plane ticket from New York to London (it cost $711). Better, she realized that her fashionable young friend Miranda Masocco of Santa Fe could accompany her. They departed on 6 June, after the writer Carl Van Vechten had given them a grand dinner party. In 1999 Miranda remembered that, dressing for the flight, Frieda wore "a Mexican blouse, a full Mexican skirt, ballet slippers, and a little Mexican beanie". Over her shoulder she had slung a huge ham bought for her son Montague. Necklaces and bracelets, made of turquoise, jangled with her every move. Much heavier now, she cut quite a figure. She cared nothing that her fellow passengers – air travellers dressed smartly in those days – found her strange. She was still Mrs D. H. Lawrence. In London she stayed with Montague and his wife, Vera; met her grandchildren; then moved to the Kingsley Hotel to see old friends such as Martin Secker, John Middleton Murry, Alexander Frere-Reeves and her trusted agent Laurence Pollinger. It was her last trip to Europe.

During the 1950s, whether in Taos or in Port Isabel, Frieda spent her days doing what she liked – writing letters after breakfast, doing household chores, making jellies or pickles in season, going to Taos's La Doña Luz restaurant for a hearty lunch with Rebecca James, Earl Stroh or Helene Wurlitzer, reading or napping or shopping in the afternoons, fixing pasta for supper, and in the evenings watching black-and-white television. It was the daily round of many retired couples, with one difference: Frieda could look forward to a stream of letters and visits from admirers of Lawrence. She had never tired of discovering what drew young people to his work.

Also in the 1950s Lawrence's work surged in popularity. After the war American veterans had migrated to college campuses, and in Britain socialist measures had encouraged the working classes to educate themselves. Alive to this social change, a publisher named Allen Lane, head of Penguin Books, gambled that good volumes, attractively printed, would sell at modest prices. In 1950 he published ten of Lawrence's novels. A further boost to Lawrence's reputation as a serious writer came both from Richard Aldington's 1950 *Portrait of a Genius, But,* an excellent biography of Lawrence based on close personal observation, and from Witter Bynner's waspish memoir of Lawrence, appearing a year later, called *Journey with Genius.* These two books showed aspects of Lawrence that Frieda had largely forgotten. "At long last I have read [your] book," she wrote to Aldington. "It was a strange experience – I forgot that it was about Lawrence [...] and about me, [I seemed] like another person. Many things, [such] as our wills clashing, I had not really grasped." She then acknowledged that, "though he bullied me, I also felt free to be myself". She was already part of a legend.

Later, a New York publisher took on an even bolder project. Barney Rosset of Grove Press, despite the objections of the Lawrence Estate, decided to publish the unexpurgated Florence edition of *Lady Chatterley's Lover* which Lawrence himself had supervised. The full unexpurgated text had never been copyrighted. Rosset wrote to Frieda in April and secured her permission. But for various reasons he delayed publishing his edition till 1959. He won the court case that ensued and, following a barrage of publicity, sold millions of copies. Similarly, a year later in England, Penguin Books, standing behind Lawrence's novel, squared off against British obscenity laws and eventually faced a jury, which returned a verdict of not guilty. Still today, on a wall at the London literary agency Pollinger Limited, hang framed copies of two royalty statements that Penguin Books issued to the Lawrence Estate. They show that sales of *Lady Chatterley's Lover* from 10 November 1960 to 30 June 1961 totalled 3,226,556 copies. The financial rewards, though they came after Frieda's death, were stupendous.

A few years earlier, before the rewards exploded, Frieda met a striking, sophisticated couple who, when they saw the manuscripts of *Lady Chatterley's Lover* that Frieda had held back, were awed. Frieda met the wife first, a sculptress named Amalia de Schulthess, whom Jake Zeitlin described as one of the most beautiful women of her generation. In 1941 she and her husband Hans had emigrated to America from Switzerland, where Hans, as the scion of an aristocratic banking family, was used to having his way. When Amalia brought him to visit Frieda in 1954, Frieda liked the homage he paid her: "Frieda *liked* good-looking young men – she liked their adulation," Amalia said. When Hans paged through the three *Lady Chatterley* manuscripts – long Frieda's most prized possession – he had to have them, and offered her $10,000. Frieda hadn't wanted to part with them, for she loved touching them and remembering the Villa Mirenda where they had been written, but she also wanted the flamboyant de Schulthesses to have them.

Frieda parted with the manuscripts just a few months after a rising institution had approached her about her selling her whole Lawrence collection. Afloat in money from oil found on government lands, the University of Texas at Austin had agreed, under the inspired leadership of Harry Ransom, Dean of Arts and Sciences, to build a humanities research centre that would house one of the world's great collections of modern literary manuscripts. Frieda was intrigued. It would be a marvellous way to honour

>─·─·─◇─·─·─<

Lawrence, and she didn't think she would "live so very much longer". There was one problem – Ravagli. Having no sentimental attachment to these manuscripts, he insisted that Dean Ransom sign a sales agreement; but, while buying everything in sight, Ransom took a cavalier attitude toward Frieda's new husband: "Angelino got worked up and wrote more harshly than he ever meant to," Frieda explained on 30 November 1954. In a draft of a letter Ravagli sent on his and Frieda's behalf, he wrote to Ransom on 24 November, insisting on a document that would "legally bind both parties" and include the "approval by the President and the Regents of the University". Without it, Ravagli believed he must "call the deal off". And so Ransom did. It was therefore the second time that an American university had missed an opportunity to buy Lawrence's manuscripts. When the University of Texas did finally acquire the *Lady Chatterley* manuscripts in 1965, the price had shot from $10,000 to $50,000 (at least half a million dollars today). Lawrence would have been amazed.

Among the last of Frieda's new friends was a young, crewcut television producer named Louis Gibbons. He liked Taos, "so quaint and beautiful"; he loved Lawrence's work; and he responded enthusiastically to Frieda, whose eyes, he wrote, were "full of young, blue, flashing fire". Later, invited to lunch in December 1954, he and his partner Thomas Young drove from Dallas, Texas, to Port Isabel, for Frieda's soup, salad, chopped venison (it was tough), ice cream and strawberries, and then went for a drive to nearby Padre Island, where Frieda, beckoning them to follow, kicked off her moccasins and ran into the shallow waves of the Gulf of Mexico. At 75, she found the smallest pleasure an adventure; her love of shared experience was inexhaustible. But in April 1956 a virus hospitalized her in Santa Fe for several days. Although warned about her health, she and Ravagli returned to Taos and normality. On 8 August, already compromised by diabetes and heavy smoking, Frieda's health collapsed.

At 11 o'clock that night she suffered a major stroke, which paralysed her right side and robbed her of speech. On 11 August – it was her 77th birthday – she died at home, surrounded by friends. Louis Gibbons arrived from Dallas two days later, just in time for the viewing of the body at a Taos funeral home and for the simple graveside service at the Lawrence Chapel. He stood with Angelo Ravagli, who would live 20 years more, mostly in Italy. As Frieda's coffin was lowered into place, William Goyen read his manly tribute to Frieda. It began, "We remember her for her rare gift of life."

As this book closes, it may be useful to put the Lawrences in perspective. For D. H. Lawrence, one of the great writers of the 20th century, marriage was the central relationship, as it was for Frieda. Detailing the struggles that both ennobled and diminished them, this book has offered a portrait of commitment and affection shaded with betrayal. Above all, it has been a portrait of love and loyalty, and the challenges they posed to a complex writer and his strong-willed wife.

As Frieda's newly published letters show, it would be a mistake to call the Lawrences' marriage exemplary or complete. Their bouts of dissension were too disturbing. It was a relationship whose essentials they had to thrash out in order to discover what was genuine in it. What was genuine was not the conventional notion of respect or deference or accommodation, but the discovery that jealousy and possessiveness complemented love and loyalty. In the spaces between them, the Lawrences tried valiantly to decode the irrational impulses that energized them. Even when it was difficult, they listened to their inner voices. Emerging from this conflicted space, they joined forces to resist the drift of their culture towards counterfeit emotion. Lawrence strongly opposed his culture; but after his death Frieda slowly reconciled herself to it – partly because she could ignore its norms. That was what money from Lawrence's books and manuscripts had finally done for her: freed her to develop her gift for friendship outside the binding structures of work.

Out of these differences in personality arose a clarity about their respective natures. If Lawrence used Frieda to help him clarify his beliefs in spontaneity and sexual discovery, she used him to refine her core of beliefs in individual freedom, in defending her worth and in embracing the recurrent rhythms of life. As Frieda allowed in a 1944 letter to Edward Gilbert, "The greatest thing he gave [me] was [...] a new joy in sex – sex as the height of all human experience." And if Lawrence saw Frieda as his road into the unconscious, where difficult new truths about the self could be found, Frieda saw Lawrence as helping her shape her immense vitality: not into proud submission to her husband (as did Achsah Brewster or Maria Huxley), nor into unchecked domination (as Mabel Luhan did), but into understanding her uniquely feminine virility. Frieda remained masculine all her life but possessed the gifts of female compassion and empathy, which she bestowed on the cluster of close friends who sustained her before and after Lawrence's death.

The Lawrences' achievement lay in their continued struggle to sort out a conflict of values that was never resolved. Lawrence's unfulfilled longings – some of them sexual – turned into deep chagrin, which he blamed for his illnesses; Frieda's dissatisfaction took the shape of a covert affair (with Ravagli), the duplicity of which she mostly dismissed. In short, their achievement allowed them eventually to discover a complex friendship, without emotional displays or sexual connections, that was at once enabling and disabling, but which fostered many days of rich contentment. However much their love was marred by disloyalty, the Lawrences believed that they enabled each other to define the core of their being (a hard place to find, for any man or woman). If they only partly succeeded, that is because deep pockets of egotism blocked them from completing themselves. They reached across the male–female divide, blended their qualities of assertion and dependence, but never fully met. What developed instead was the crosscut of temperaments that exposed the Lawrences' mutual affection and antagonism, stimulation and peace.

To see Lawrence and Frieda "whole" requires us to admit the erosion of love and loyalty in the later years of their marriage. Their loss of emotional coherence after 1925 meant that Frieda would later need to engage in *recovering* Lawrence. After his death, she very soon found a sustained commitment to his memory that she could pursue for the rest of her life. Her love grew simpler and purer, the longer Lawrence was dead. Although her respect and affection for Angelo Ravagli, her third husband, cannot be doubted, it did not rival her passion for Lawrence. Metaphorically, Lawrence built Frieda a room that Ravagli later furnished.

There is, at the close, a reason for rediscovering the essence of the Lawrence legend. It is that the Lawrences interpreted the tensions of 20th-century life as few have done. They tested the barriers to love and work, reconceptualized the nature of friendship and redefined the boundaries of so-called purity. In so doing, they found that at the far side of risk lay meaning, significance and – at times – moments of intense revelation. For that, readers of modern literature will long remember them.

Notes

Quotations in my text are cited below by page reference, followed by key words of quotation and their source, published or unpublished. Abbreviations include:

DHL: D. H. Lawrence

DHL Letters: The Letters of D. H. Lawrence, 8 volumes, various editors (Cambridge: Cambridge University Press, 1979–2000). Volume and page number follow each citation.

FL: Frieda Lawrence

HRHRC: Harry Ransom Humanities Research Center, University of Texas at Austin

sütterlin: Letter written in *sütterlin*, transcribed and translated by John Worthen and Constance Rumpf-Worthen. Numbers (e.g. *sütterlin* 37) refer to the Worthens' numbering of 93 letters in *sütterlin*, an old-fashioned German script that Frieda learned at school. The letters are held at HRHRC.

Preface

1   "plucky soul": FL to Dr. Andrew Morland, [c. 4 March 1930]; quoted in James T. Boulton, ed., "Further Letters of D. H. Lawrence," *Journal of D. H. Lawrence Studies* 1.1 (2006): 32.

2   "a thousand [. . .] human beings": unpublished letter, FL to Friedel Gross, ?30 Sept. 1913, *sütterlin* 37.

3   "keep her": *DHL Letters* i 427, 18 July 1912, to Edward Garnett.

3   "Frieda and [. . .] more unified": *DHL Letters* ii 539, 15 Feb. 1916, to Ottoline Morrell.

3 "wrong in it": unpublished letter, FL to Sallie Hopkin, 25 Dec. 1912, University of Nottingham; quoted in Michael Squires and Lynn K. Talbot, *Living at the Edge: A Biography of D. H. Lawrence and Frieda von Richthofen* (Madison: University of Wisconsin Press, 2002): 64. Hereafter cited as *Living at the Edge*.

4 "have everything": unpublished letter, FL to Ottoline Morrell, [1934]; cited in Christie's Auction Catalog, 1 Nov. 2006.

4 "in a lifetime!": unpublished letter, 12 July 1956, FL to Rolf Gardiner; quoted in *Living at the Edge* 412.

4 "male dove!": unpublished letter, FL to Edgar Jaffe, c. 8 Feb. 1914, *sütterlin* 38.

Chapter 1, "Two Lonely People"

6 "a lifetime": *DHL Letters* i 384, 17 April 1912, to Edward Garnett.

6 "and ourselves": Frieda Lawrence, *Not I, But the Wind* (New York: Viking, 1934): 7. Hereafter cited as *Not I, But the Wind*.

7 "are right": *DHL Letters* i 403–4, 15 and 16 May 1912, to Frieda Weekley.

8 "so hard": *DHL Letters* i 421, 3 July 1912, to Edward Garnett.

8 "filthy hound": *DHL Letters* i 484, 5 Dec. 1912, to David Garnett.

8 "each other": *DHL Letters* i 420, 3 July 1912, to Edward Garnett.

9 "is love": *DHL Letters* i 440, 19 Aug. 1912, to Sallie Hopkin.

9 "gloomy millennia": Letter A, *The Otto Gross–Frieda Weekley Correspondence*, ed. John Turner et al., *D. H. Lawrence Review* 22 (1990): 165 (emphasis removed). Hereafter cited as *Gross–Weekley Correspondence*.

10 "things around": *DHL Letters* i 503, 17 Jan. 1913, to Ernest Collings.

10 "indescribably beautiful!": unpublished letter, FL to Anna von Richthofen, ?15 Sept. 1912, *sütterlin* 31.

Chapter 2, "Eastwood and Metz"

11 "flowers bloom": Frieda Lawrence, *Not I, But the Wind* 43.

11 "like life": *DHL Letters* i 477, 19 Nov. 1912, to Edward Garnett.

11 "so plucky [. . .] you down": *DHL Letters* i 479, 19 Nov. 1912, to Edward Garnett.

12 "with laughter": *Not I, But the Wind* 44.

12 "to eat": Dorothy Brett, *Lawrence and Brett, A Friendship* (Philadelphia: Lippincott, 1933): 279.

13 "bright in his manner": quoted in John Worthen, *D. H. Lawrence: The Early Years* (Cambridge: Cambridge University Press, 1991): 118.

14 "was exquisite": D. H. Lawrence, "The White Stocking," in *The Prussian Officer and Other Stories*, ed. John Worthen (Cambridge: Cambridge University Press, 1983): 153. The passage quoted was revised in 1914.

14 "his studies": Jessie Chambers, *D. H. Lawrence: A Personal Record by E. T.* (London: Cape, 1936; New York: Knight, 1936): 75.

14 "debasing struggle": *DHL Letters* i 93, 16 Nov. 1908, to Louisa Burrows.

15 "invincible spear": "Death-Paean of a Mother," *Guardian*, 9 Nov. 1990.

15 "be alone": *DHL Letters* i 285, 12 July 1911, to Helen Corke.

16 "but sorrow": *DHL Letters* i 291, [19 July 1911], to Louisa Burrows.

16 "believed in me": quoted in *Lawrence and Brett* 258.

17 "be here": FL to Else von Richthofen, 21 Feb. 1898, in *Frieda Lawrence: The Memoirs and Correspondence*, ed. E. W. Tedlock, Jr. (New York: Knopf, 1964): 143. Hereafter cited as *Memoirs and Correspondence*.

17 "I am [. . .] with him": unpublished letter, FL to Else von Richthofen, n.d. [1898], *sütterlin* 5.

17 "wonderland of love": Letter Q, summer 1907, *Gross–Weekley Correspondence* 194.

18 "to church": Letter R, summer 1907, *Gross–Weekley Correspondence* 194.

Chapter 3, "Paradise"

19 "beyond belief": D. H. Lawrence, *Twilight in Italy and Other Essays*, ed. Paul Eggert (Cambridge: Cambridge University Press, 1994): 154.

19 "unthinkable [. . .] of love": unpublished letter, FL to Else von Richthofen, 2 Nov. 1912, *sütterlin* 32.

19 "the children": *DHL Letters* i 521, 27 Feb. 1913, to David Garnett.

19 "committed adultery": *DHL Letters* i 524, 5 March 1913, to Arthur McLeod.

20 "against Frieda": *DHL Letters* i 532, 25 March 1913, to Ada Lawrence.

20 "difficult and unpleasant": *DHL Letters* i 538, 5 April 1913, to Ada Lawrence.

20 "Mrs Lawrence": *DHL Letters* ii 22, [14 June 1913], to Miss Whale.

21 "about me": Edward Nehls, comp., *D. H. Lawrence: A Composite Biography*, vol. i (Madison: University of Wisconsin Press, 1957): 200. Hereafter cited as *A Composite Biography* followed by volume number.

21 "go far": *DHL Letters* ii 49–50, 22 July 1913, to Else von Richthofen.

21 "quite unbelievable": unpublished letter, FL to Else von Richthofen, 30 Sept. 1913, *sütterlin* 37.

21 "the slums": *ibid*.

22 "one want?": *ibid*.

22 "are uncharted": Virginia Woolf, *Jacob's Room* (1922; reprinted San Diego: Harcourt Brace, n.d.): 94.

22 "it is like": *DHL Letters* ii 82, 6 Oct. 1913, to Edward Garnett.

23 "I know": *DHL Letters* ii 125, 18 Dec. 1913, to William Hopkin.

23 "little place": unpublished letter, FL to Henry Savage, [19 Jan. 1914], Stanford University.

23 "is here": unpublished letter, FL to Edgar Jaffe, [c. 8 Feb. 1914], *sütterlin* 38.

23 "sloppy [. . .] inartistic": quoted in *Living at the Edge* 90.

23 "of infinity": D. H. Lawrence, *The Rainbow*, ed. Mark Kinkead-Weekes (Cambridge: Cambridge University Press, 1989): 409.

24 "registrar's office": *DHL Letters* ii 196, 13 July 1914, to Sallie Hopkin.

Chapter 4, "My Heart Is Smashed"

25 "all unnaturalized [. . .] camps": *Times*, 23 Oct. 1914, p. 4.

26 "very happy together": quoted in *Living at the Edge* 81.

26 "great passion": *DHL Letters* ii 253 n4, 30 Dec. 1914, Ottoline Morrell to Bertrand Russell.

26 "German soldiers": quoted in *A Composite Biography* i 250–51. The excerpt is drawn from Compton Mackenzie's novel *The South Wind of Love* (1937); in 1953 he claimed that the novel's characterization of Lawrence and Frieda was "conversationally exact" (*A Composite Biography* i 570).

26 "colossal idiocy!": *DHL Letters* ii 212, 5 Sept. 1914, to James B. Pinker.

27 "in this world!": unpublished letter, [c. 19 March 1915], FL to Ottoline Morrell, HRHRC.

27 "highly sexed": The observer is Leonard Woolf; see his *Downhill All the Way: An Autobiography of the Years 1919–1939* (London: Hogarth Press, 1967; New York: Harcourt Brace Jovanovich, 1967): 102.

27 "a great lady": *DHL Letters* ii 281, [11 Feb. 1915], to Ottoline Morrell.

28 "may have been": unpublished letter, FL to Ottoline Morrell, [2 Aug. 1915], HRHRC.

28 "traitor to her": *DHL Letters* ii 462, 3 Dec. 1915, to Ottoline Morrell.

28 "her influence": *Not I, But the Wind 82.*

28 "I have been [. . .] with him": quoted in Mark Kinkead-Weekes, *D. H. Lawrence: Triumph to Exile* (Cambridge: Cambridge University Press, 1996): 240.

29 "terribly beautiful": D. H. Lawrence, *The Rainbow* 220.

30 "scratch the door": *DHL Letters* ii 293, 24 Feb. 1915, to James B. Pinker.

30 One night he dreamed: *DHL Letters* ii 346, [25 May 1915], to Ottoline Morrell.

30 the American edition: Benjamin Huebsch published an expurgated edition of *The Rainbow* in New York, 30 November 1915. The expurgations did not have Lawrence's approval.

30 "defiance of [. . .] exceptional strength": Unsigned review in the *Standard*, reprinted in R. P. Draper, ed., *D. H. Lawrence: The Critical Heritage* (London: Routledge & Kegan Paul, 1970; New York: Barnes & Noble, 1970): 90.

30 "wind of war": James Douglas in the *Star*, reprinted in Draper, *D. H. Lawrence 93–4.*

31 "a thousand fragments": *DHL Letters* ii 454, 28 Nov. 1915, to Cynthia Asquith.

31 "destruction and misery": *DHL Letters* ii 450, 22 Nov. 1915, to Ottoline Morrell.

Chapter 5, "A Map of Passion"

32 "I love it": *DHL Letters* ii 492, 31 Dec. 1915, to Catherine Carswell.

32 "about it – ": unpublished letter, [9 Jan. 1916], FL to Ottoline Morrell, HRHRC.

32 "for revenge": unpublished letter, [17 Jan. 1916], FL to Ottoline Morrell, HRHRC.

32 "wintry inflammation": *DHL Letters* ii 503, [11 Jan. 1916], to Catherine Carswell.

33 whispered something else: John Worthen however believes that in 1916 Lawrence did not have TB; see Worthen, *D. H. Lawrence: The Life of an Outsider* (London: Allen Lane, 2005; New York: Overlook, 2005): 184.

33 "a great strain [. . .] unbearable": unpublished letter, [9 Jan. 1916], FL to Ottoline Morrell, HRHRC.

34 "he has done": unpublished letter, 11 July 1916, FL to E. M. Forster, King's College Library, Cambridge.

34 "intellectual decomposition": *DHL Letters* ii 642, [c. 20 Aug. 1916], to Barbara Low.

34 "a brigand": *DHL Letters* ii 542, 17 Feb. 1916, to Katherine Mansfield and John Middleton Murry.

34 "bombs": *DHL Letters* ii 547, [19 Feb. 1916], to Bertrand Russell.

35 "secret cruelty": D. H. Lawrence, *The First "Women in Love"*, ed. John Worthen and Lindeth Vasey (Cambridge: Cambridge University Press, 1998): 223.

35 "physical being": *The First "Women in Love"* 247.

35 "great shock": quoted in *Ottoline at Garsington: Memoirs of Lady Ottoline Morrell 1915–1918*, ed. Robert Gathorne-Hardy (London: Faber, 1974): 128.

36 "filth": *DHL Letters* iii 53, [15 Dec. 1916], to S. S. Koteliansky.

36 "loathing" for him: *DHL Letters* iii 83, 25 Jan. 1917, to Gordon Campbell.

36 "you were here": *DHL Letters* iii 127, 23 May 1917, to John Middleton Murry.

36 "against me": *DHL Letters* ii 667, 15 Oct. 1916, to S. S. Koteliansky.

37 "the initiated": *DHL Letters* iii 180, [7 Nov. 1917], to Cecil Gray.

37 "central secrets [of life]": *The First "Women in Love"* 414.

37 "evil face": *DHL Letters* ii 566, 6 March 1916, to Dollie Radford.

Chapter 6, "Banished from Cornwall"

39 "all about": *DHL Letters* iii 167, 12 Oct. 1917, to Cecil Gray.

40 "smart things": D. H. Lawrence, *Aaron's Rod*, ed. Mara Kalnins (Cambridge: Cambridge University Press, 1988): 164.

40 "cracked for ever": *DHL Letters* iii 329, [28 Feb. 1919], to S. S. Koteliansky.

41 "terrifying lust": D. H. Lawrence, "Tickets Please," in *England, My England and Other Stories*, ed. Bruce Steele (Cambridge: Cambridge University Press, 1990): 44.

41 "travelling grasp": D. H. Lawrence, "The Blind Man," in *England, My England and Other Stories*, ed. Bruce Steele (Cambridge: Cambridge University Press, 1990): 62.

41 "shell is broken": "The Blind Man" 63.

41 "old people": *DHL Letters* iii 222, 12 March 1918, to William Hopkin.

42 "to sing again": Enid Hopkin Hilton, *More than One Life: A Nottinghamshire Childhood with D. H. Lawrence* (Dover, NH: Alan Sutton, 1993): 31–2.

42 "one big curse": unpublished letter, FL to William Hopkin, 30 Dec. 1918, Nottinghamshire Archives; quoted in *Living at the Edge* 186.

43 "at margarine": *DHL Letters* iii 335, 10 March 1919, to Beatrice Campbell.

43 "for us all": *DHL Letters* iii 347, 5 April 1919, to Amy Lowell.

43 "a new country": *DHL Letters* iii 331, 2 March 1919, to Harriet Monroe.

43 "its complications": *DHL Letters* iii 333, 6 March 1919, to Cynthia Asquith.

44   "I believe": *DHL Letters* iii 337, [14 March 1919], to S. S. Koteliansky.

44   "too much married": quoted in *A Composite Biography* i 503.

45   "at D. H.": quoted in *A Composite Biography* i 504–5.

Chapter 7, "Awakening in Italy"

46   "very hungry": FL to Cynthia Asquith, [1 July 1919], *Memoirs and Correspondence* 214; quoted from ms.

46   "as possible": *DHL Letters* iii 367, 30 June 1919, to S. S. Koteliansky.

47   "for [my] health": *DHL Letters* iii 401, 30 Sept. 1919, to Benjamin Huebsch.

47   "his best": quoted in *Modern Fiction Studies* (24) 1978: 366.

47   "state of animosity": quoted in *A Composite Biography* i 507.

48   "sun and sea": *DHL Letters* iii 416, 17 Nov. 1919, to Rosalind Baynes.

49   "a very sexual person": quoted in Louise E. Wright, "Talk about Real Men: Jack London's Correspondence with Maurice Magnus," *Journal of Popular Culture* 40 (2007): 367. Letter of 19 Nov. 1911.

49   "bisexual types": letter, Maurice Magnus to Norman Douglas, 18 July 1920; quoted in Brenda Maddox, *D. H. Lawrence: The Story of a Marriage* (New York: Simon & Schuster, 1994): 269.

49   "town to me": *Not I, But the Wind* 98.

49   "go south": *DHL Letters* iii 424, [28 Dec. 1919], to Rosalind Baynes.

50   "extremely beautiful": *DHL Letters* iii 442, 4 Jan. 1920, to Catherine Carswell.

50   "the Tarantella": FL to Violet Monk, 6 Jan. 1920, *Memoirs and Correspondence* 215–16; ms. punctuation adopted.

50   "selfconscious effort": *DHL Letters* iii 443, 4 Jan. 1920, to Catherine Carswell.

50   "immensely": *DHL Letters* iii 455, 12 Jan. 1920, to Max Plowman.

50   "beautiful beyond words": *DHL Letters* iii 454, 12 Jan. 1920, to Violet Monk.

51   "wings of [his] soul": *DHL Letters* iii 522, [10 May 1920], to Compton Mackenzie.

Chapter 8, "Intoxication"

52   "very much": unpublished postcard, FL to Margaret King, postmarked 27 March 1920, University of Nottingham.

52   "better than Capri": *DHL Letters* iii 489, 20 March 1920, to Fritz Krenkow.

53   "north again": *DHL Letters* iii 511, 29 April 1920, to S. S. Koteliansky.

53   "Of life": D. H. Lawrence, *Birds, Beasts and Flowers* (1923; reprinted Santa Rosa, CA: Black Sparrow Press, 1992): 131.

53   "end of August": *DHL Letters* iii 575, [22 July 1920], to Rosalind Baynes.

54   "it is autumn": *DHL Letters* iii 581, 30 July 1920, to Hilda Brown.

54   "most people [. . .] to bed": Rosalind Thornycroft, *Time Which Spaces Us Apart* (Batscombe, Somerset: privately printed, 1991): 78–9.

54   "meet next": *DHL Letters* iii 609, [7 Oct. 1920], to Rosalind Baynes.

55   "groove [. . .] the scarlet": *Birds, Beasts and Flowers* 15–19.

55   "black hole": *Birds, Beasts and Flowers* 129.

55   "A kiss [. . .] of loneliness": *Birds, Beasts and Flowers* 23–4.

56   "his privacy ferociously": *Not I, But the Wind* 115. John Worthen believes that Frieda "found out" about the affair and was angry (see his *D. H. Lawrence: The Life of an Outsider* 234).

56   "blasted [. . .] vital tissue": D. H. Lawrence, *Aaron's Rod* 263.

56   "lifted-upness": *DHL Letters* iii 613, 18 Oct. 1920, to Robert Mountsier.

56   "like spring": FL to Irene and Percy Whittley, in *DHL Letters* iii 615, [23 Oct. 1920].

56   "shall *love* it – ": unpublished letter, FL to Robert Mountsier, [2 Jan. 1921], Northwestern University.

57   "an oyster shell": D. H. Lawrence, *Sea and Sardinia*, ed. Mara Kalnins (Cambridge: Cambridge University Press, 1997): 10.

57   "over parsnips": *Sea and Sardinia* 13.

57   "like pressed leaves": *Sea and Sardinia* 41.

57   "Suddenly [. . .] jeering insolence": *Sea and Sardinia* 24.

57   "wooden hearts": *Sea and Sardinia* 35.

57   "male life": *Sea and Sardinia* 129.

58 *"das Glück"*: Benjamin Huebsch to D. H. Lawrence, in *DHL Letters* iv 229 n2, 3 March 1922.

58 "starting for America – ": unpublished letter, FL to Robert Mountsier, 5 Feb. 1921, Northwestern University.

58 "I should [. . .] Thrasher's farm": *DHL Letters* iii 661, 5 Feb. 1921, to Robert Mountsier.

58 "to Thrasher's Farm": unpublished account, "Moneys Received and Expended by Robert Mountsier, Acting as Agent for D. H. Lawrence, March 16 to April 26, 1921", Copley Library. By comparison the *Dial* paid Lawrence $30 for his poem "Snake."

59 "find my direction": *DHL Letters* iii 689, 22 March 1921, to Robert Mountsier.

59 "crisis for me": *DHL Letters* iii 693, [25 March 1921], to Robert Mountsier.

59 "my plan": *DHL Letters* iii 683, [15 March 1921], to Mary Cannan.

Chapter 9, "East and West"

60 "look back": *DHL Letters* viii 53, [23 Feb. 1922], to Anna von Richthofen.

60 "devil of a journey": *DHL Letters* iii 706, [28 April 1921], to John Ellingham Brooks.

61 "tactful touch": Earl and Achsah Brewster, *D. H. Lawrence: Reminiscences and Correspondence* (London: Secker, 1934): 14.

62 "eye of love": *DHL Letters* iii 734, 3 June 1921, to Evelyn Scott.

62 "shudder[s] . . . such love again": D. H. Lawrence, "The Captain's Doll," in *The Fox, The Captain's Doll, The Ladybird*, ed. Dieter Mehl (Cambridge: Cambridge University Press, 1992): 115.

63 "he answered": "The Captain's Doll" 130.

63 "I want [. . .] but love": "The Captain's Doll" 150–51.

63 "blissfully happy": *DHL Letters* viii 45, [25 Aug. 1921], to Anna von Richthofen.

63 "is heaven": *DHL Letters* iv 92, [30 Sept. 1921], to Irene Whittley.

63 "own house": *DHL Letters* iv 95, [8 Oct. 1921], to Robert Mountsier.

64 "early spring": *DHL Letters* iv 80, 29 Aug. 1921, to Robert Mountsier.

64 "from the Pacific": *DHL Letters* iv 95, 8 Oct. 1921, to Earl Brewster.

64 "angrier I become": DHL Letters iv 98, 12 Oct. 1921, to Violet Monk.

64 "to Ceylon": *DHL Letters* iv 110, 2 Nov. 1921, to Earl Brewster.

64 "I want to go": *DHL Letters* iv 125, 16 Nov. 1921, to Earl Brewster.

65 "east and west": *DHL Letters* iv 170–71, 18 Jan. 1922, to Earl Brewster.

65 "strong enough": FL to Mabel Dodge Luhan, 26 Jan. 1922, in *DHL Letters* iv 181 n4.

Chapter 10, "Assorted Animals"

67 "round the world": unpublished letter, FL to Anna von Richthofen, 20 May 1922, *sütterlin* 44.

68 "rather lovely really": *DHL Letters* iv 208, 4 March 1922, to Norman Douglas.

68 "this way": *DHL Letters* iv 212, [7 March 1922], to Anna von Richthofen.

68 "if you walk a few yards": *DHL Letters* iv 216, 24 March 1922, to Emily King.

68 infected with malaria: David Ellis believes that Lawrence may have been infected in Sicily shortly before he sailed for Ceylon. See Ellis, *D. H. Lawrence: Dying Game 1922–1930* (Cambridge: Cambridge University Press, 1998): 611 n2.

68 "can't stand Ceylon": *DHL Letters* iv 222, [3 April 1922], to Anna Jenkins.

68 "dead off" Buddhism: *DHL Letters* iv 218, 28 March 1922, to Anna Jenkins.

68 to Buddha "hideous": *DHL Letters* iv 221, 3 April 1922, to Mary Cannan.

68 "the tropics": *DHL Letters* iv 223, [3 April 1922], to Else Jaffe.

69 sick "all the time": *DHL Letters* iv 225, [8 April 1922], to Anna Jenkins

69 "THIRROUL [. . .] Winter T[er]ms": quoted in Joseph Davis, *D. H. Lawrence at Thirroul* (Sydney: Collins, 1989): 32.

69 "The heavy [. . .] very comfortable": *DHL Letters* iv 249, 30 May 1922, to Anna von Richthofen.

70 "Here we sit [. . .] every day": unpublished letter, FL to Anna von Richthofen, 22 June 1922, *sütterlin* 45.

70 "his dearest book – very striking": unpublished letter, FL to Anna von Richthofen, 7 July 1922, *sütterlin* 45.

70 "a glamour like magic": D. H. Lawrence, *Kangaroo*, ed. Bruce Steele (Cambridge: Cambridge University Press, 1994): 70.

71 "said he bitingly": *Kangaroo* 69–70.

71 "carry him into action": *Kangaroo* 143.

71 "I've *ever* known": *Kangaroo* 356.

71 A photograph taken at this time: photograph by William Forrester located at the Wollongong City Library, Australia.

72 "important for us!": unpublished letter, FL to Else Jaffe, [31 July 1922], *sütterlin* 46.

72 "growing all the time": unpublished letter, FL to Anna von Richthofen, 9 Aug. 1922, *sütterlin* 47.

72 over $4,000: the figure Thomas Seltzer quoted was $4,286.46; letter of 1 February 1923, Seltzer to DHL, in Jay A. Gertzman and Michael Squires, "New Letters from Thomas Seltzer and Robert Mountsier to D. H. Lawrence," *DHL Review* 28 (1999): 65.

72 "astonishingly famous": unpublished letter, FL to Anna von Richthofen, [c. 14 Sept. 1922], *sütterlin* 49.

72 a cheque for $30: D. H. Lawrence, check no. 5, Charleroi [Pennsylvania] Savings & Trust Co., unpublished checkbook 1922–1923, Fray Angélico Chávez History Library, Santa Fe, New Mexico (hereafter cited as Chávez). From this checking account Lawrence sent his mother-in-law a further $25 on 5 December 1922 (check no. 12) and the same amount on 3 February 1923 (check no. 15).

72 "latest fashion": unpublished letter, FL to Anna von Richthofen, [31 July 1922], *sütterlin* 46.

Chapter 11, "Mountains in America"

74 "on the go": *DHL Letters* iv 309, 25 Sept. 1922, to William Siebenhaar.

74 "I believe it": unpublished letter, FL to Anna von Richthofen, [c. 14 Sept. 1922], *sütterlin* 49.

75 "isn't happy here": unpublished letter, FL to Anna von Richthofen, [c. 9 Nov. 1922], *sütterlin* 50.

75 "heal Lawrence completely": unpublished letter, FL to Anna von Richthofen, [c. 14 Sept. 1922], *sütterlin* 49.

75 living there "alone": *DHL Letters* iv 329, 25 Oct. 1922, to Robert Mountsier.

75 "go and live there": *DHL Letters* iv 333, [31 Oct. 1922], to Elizabeth Freeman.

75 "Spanish with Sabino": unpublished letter, FL to Anna von Richthofen, [c. 9 Nov. 1922], *sütterlin* 50.

76 "embracing syphilitics": quoted in Armin Arnold, *D. H. Lawrence and America* (New York: Philosophical Library, 1959): 90.

76 "thing in my life": *DHL Letters* iv 337, 7 Nov. 1922, to S. S. Koteliansky.

76 "very different [here]": *DHL Letters* iv 349, 4 Dec. 1922, to S. S. Koteliansky.

77 "veal and pork as we want": FL to Anna von Richthofen, [8 Dec. 1922], in *DHL Letters* iv 357; I cite the Worthens' translation (*sütterlin* 51).

77 "was so well!": unpublished letter, FL to Anna von Richthofen, 9 Jan. 1923, *sütterlin* 52.

77 "impudent" and "meddling": Gertzman and Squires, "New Letters from Thomas Seltzer and Robert Mountsier" 61.

78 "ever did was helpful": Thomas Seltzer, letter of 3 March 1923, in Gertzman and Squires, "New Letters from Thomas Seltzer and Robert Mountsier" 73.

78 that "liar" Mabel: *DHL Letters* iv 372, 24 Jan. 1923, to Elizabeth Freeman.

78 "did not believe in me": *DHL Letters* iv 382, 10 Feb. 1923, to Thomas Seltzer.

78 "can't stand any more": *DHL Letters* iv 378, 7 Feb. 1923, to Thomas Seltzer.

78 "To me, loyalty [comes] far before love": *DHL Letters* iv 368, 4 Jan. 1923, to Thomas Seltzer.

78 "I know I can love": FL to S. S. Koteliansky, 4 Dec. 1923; quoted in *Memoirs and Correspondence* 225.

78 "are really tiring": unpublished letter, FL to Anna von Richthofen, 2 Feb. 1923, *sütterlin* 53.

79 "a good time together": *DHL Letters* iv 388, [16? Feb. 1923], to Willard Johnson.

79 Lawrence had invited five people: Merrild, Götzsche, Bynner, Johnson, and Mabel's friend Elizabeth Freeman.

79 "almost perfect" for tubercular types: T. Philip Terry, *Terry's Guide to Mexico,* revised edn (Boston: Houghton Mifflin, 1923): xxvi.

Chapter 12, "Oaxacan Mysteries"

80 "country down there": Witter Bynner, *Journey with Genius: Recollections and Reflections concerning the D. H. Lawrences* (New York: John Day, 1951; London: Peter Nevill, 1953): 17.

80 "vile and degraded": FL to Adele Seltzer, 8 April 1923; quoted in *D. H. Lawrence: Letters to Thomas and Adele Seltzer,* ed. Gerald M. Lacy (Santa Barbara, CA: Black Sparrow Press, 1976): 88. Hereafter cited as *Letters to Thomas and Adele Seltzer.*

81 "savage underneath": *DHL Letters* iv 442, 9 May 1923, to Thomas Seltzer.

81 "we may settle": *DHL Letters* iv 430, [21 April 1923], to Kai Götzsche and Knud Merrild.

81 "TAKE EVENING TRAIN": *DHL Letters* iv 435, [1 May 1923], to Frieda Lawrence.

81 "thing he ever did": FL to Adele Seltzer, 10 June 1923, *DHL Letters* iv 455.

82 "in love with nobody": D. H. Lawrence, *Quetzalcoatl: The Early Version of "The Plumed Serpent,"* ed. Louis L. Martz (Redding Ridge, CT: Black Swan Books, 1995): 31. Hereafter cited as *Quetzalcoatl.*

82 "Mysterious" and "not quite fathomable": *Quetzalcoatl* 20.

82 "wildness [was] undreamt of": unpublished letter, FL to Anna von Richthofen,[10 June 1923], *sütterlin* 57.

82 "above all love": *Quetzalcoatl* 34.

82 "other novel of mine": *DHL Letters* iv 457, 15 June 1923, to Thomas Seltzer.

83 "spell [. . .] in her heart": *Quetzalcoatl* 160.

83 "all through her body": *Quetzalcoatl* 300.

83 "to go back to Europe": *DHL Letters* iv 458, 15 June 1923, to Thomas Seltzer.

84 "desolate inside": *DHL Letters* iv 473, 25? July 1923, to Willard Johnson.

84   *"she* will sail [to England] on the 18th": *DHL Letters* iv 478, 7 Aug. 1923, to S. S. Koteliansky; italics mine.

84   "on the old ground": *DHL Letters* iv 480, 7 Aug. 1923, to John Middleton Murry.

84   "with a cheerful soul": *DHL Letters* iv 483, 13 Aug. 1923, to John Middleton Murry.

84   "honorable manhood in them": *DHL Letters* iv 463, [27 June 1923], to Knud Merrild.

84   "Norse gods [. . .] taste": Adele Seltzer to Dorothy Hoskins, 7 Jan. 1923; Adele Seltzer to her sisters, 16 Jan. 1923; quoted in *Letters to Thomas and Adele Seltzer* 251, 187.

85   "help us manage [a little banana farm]": *DHL Letters* iv 459, [17 June 1923], to Kai Götzsche and Knud Merrild.

85   "we could make a life": *DHL Letters* iv 470, 15 July 1923, to Kai Götzsche and Knud Merrild.

85   "go packing among the mountains": *DHL Letters* iv 481, 7 Aug. 1923, to Knud Merrild.

85   building a life together: see FL to Kai Götzsche and Knud Merrild, [17 June 1923], *DHL Letters* iv 459.

85   "I feel [. . .] wrote him so": FL to Adele Seltzer, 26? Aug. 1923, in *Letters to Thomas and Adele Seltzer* 106.

85   "a group, a family, a circle of friends": *Quetzalcoatl* 32.

Chapter 13, "A Ship Goes East"

87   "looks at [. . .] an onlooker": *DHL Letters* iv 507, [5 Oct. 1923], to Knud Merrild.

87   "difficult to live with": Knud Merrild, *With D. H. Lawrence in New Mexico: A Memoir of D. H. Lawrence* (1938; reprinted London: Routledge, 1964): 343.

88   "casual," without deep affection: Bynner, *Journey with Genius* 194.

88   "It's time [. . .] very safe": *DHL Letters* viii 85, 22 Sept. 1923, DHL to FL.

88   "within six months": *Los Angeles Times*, 19 Sept. 1923, section A: 1.

88   "safe hidden somewhere": *DHL Letters* viii 85, 22 Sept. 1923, DHL to FL.

88   "must come back": *DHL Letters* iv 513, 17 Oct. 1923, to Catherine Carswell.

88   "alien": *DHL Letters* iv 519, 22 Oct. 1923, to S. S. Koteliansky.

89　"an important female": FL to Adele Seltzer, 2 Sept. 1923, in *Letters to Thomas and Adele Seltzer* 108.

89　Lawrence could have spared a couple of thousand dollars for it: In September 1923 DHL carried a balance of $590.90 in his Charleroi Trust account (Chávez). In 1922 he earned $4,250 in net income, and in June 1923 Seltzer paid him a further $4,306 (*DHL Letters* iv 464), then another $1,000 on 15 August 1923 (*DHL Letters* v 18 n4).

89　"I do hope [. . .] go to it": unpublished letter, FL to Martin Secker, 8 Oct. 1923, HRHRC.

89　"for eliciting emotion in others": Catherine Carswell, *The Savage Pilgrimage: A Narrative of D. H. Lawrence* (London: Chatto and Windus, 1932): 193.

89　"that Lawrence [. . .] than you": FL to Adele Seltzer, 2 Sept. 1923, in *Letters to Thomas and Adele Seltzer* 108.

90　"very tall [. . .] absolutely distinguished": unpublished letter, FL to Anna von Richthofen, [?22 Sept. 1923], *sütterlin* 61.

90　"terribly attached [. . .] I am here": unpublished letter, FL to Anna von Richthofen, 24 Dec. 1923, *sütterlin* 64.

90　"than I had dreamed": unpublished letter, FL to Anna von Richthofen, [? 9 Jan. 1924], *sütterlin* 65.

90　Frieda and Murry may have become lovers: Recent evidence for an affair is cited in Hignett, *Brett* 138; recent evidence against it, in Worthen, *Outsider* 297. See also *Living at the Edge* 462n.

90　"very much": unpublished letter, FL to Anna von Richthofen, 5 Nov. 1923, *sütterlin* 62.

91　"should not [. . .] in Mexico": *Not I, But the Wind* 144.

91　"brought me here": *DHL Letters* iv 544, [17 Dec. 1923], to Idella Purnell.

91　"the greatness of Lawrence": Carswell, *A Savage Pilgrimage* 209.

91　"no part or place": *ibid.* 212.

91　"still and unresponsive": *ibid.* 212.

91　"eschew emotions – they are a disease": *DHL Letters* iv 581, 13 Feb. 1924, to John Middleton Murry.

92　pregnant with Murry's child: For the evidence see Hignett 136.

92　"Taos is about the best place": *DHL Letters* iv 539, 19 Nov. 1923, to Mabel Dodge Luhan.

92　"subtle, cunning homage": D. H. Lawrence, "The Border-

Line," in *The Woman Who Rode Away and Other Stories*,
ed. Dieter Mehl and Christa Jansohn (Cambridge: Cambridge
University Press, 1995): 81.

92 "And dimly [. . .] own contentment": "The Border-Line" 86.

93 "out of here": *DHL Letters* iv 544, [17 Dec. 1923], to Thomas
Seltzer.

93 he often put off writing important letters: In their biographical
account of the Seltzers, Alexandra Lee Levin and Lawrence
L. Levin explain that Thomas was "congenitally unable to do
anything on time" (*Letters to Thomas and Adele Seltzer* 191).

93 "loyal to you": letter of 26 Jan. 1923, in Gertzman and Squires,
"New Letters from Thomas Seltzer and Robert Mountsier"
59.

Chapter 14, "Frieda's Pine Woods"

94 "in the bank": *DHL Letters* v 18, [16 March 1924], to
Catherine Carswell.

94 "inexpressibly": *DHL Letters* v 22, 4 April 1924, to Mollie
Skinner.

94 "depression": *DHL Letters* v 26, 4 April 1924, to Curtis
Brown.

94 "growing lively again": *DHL Letters* v 24, 4 April 1924, to
Martin Secker.

95 "essentially a fighter": *DHL Letters* v 67, 4 July 1924, to Rolf
Gardiner.

95 "grotesque [. . .] and English": Mabel Luhan, *Lorenzo in Taos*
(New York: Knopf, 1932): 191.

95 "a real odd man out": Carswell, *A Savage Pilgrimage* 200.

96 "fifty thousand dollars": unpublished letter, FL to Anna von
Richthofen, [c. 15 July 1924], *sütterlin* 66. That was an inflated
estimate. In 1937 Frieda's complete collection of Lawrence's
manuscripts was offered to Harvard University for $25,000:
see Michael Squires, ed., *D. H. Lawrence's Manuscripts: The
Correspondence of Frieda Lawrence, Jake Zeitlin, and Others*
(Basingstoke: Macmillan, 1991; New York: St. Martin's, 1991):
85–7. Hereafter cited as *D. H. Lawrence's Manuscripts*.

96 "great fun": *DHL Letters* v 48, [26 May 1924], to Thomas
Seltzer.

97 "simple and stylish": unpublished letter, FL to Anna von
Richthofen, 8 Aug. 1924, *sütterlin* 67.

97 "very economical": *DHL Letters* v 45, 18 May 1924, to Thomas Seltzer.

97 "that really is America": *DHL Letters* v 63, 28 June 1924, to Anna von Richthofen.

98 "pristine race": quoted in Knud Merrild, *With D. H. Lawrence in New Mexico: A Memoir of D. H. Lawrence* (1938; reprinted London: Routledge, 1964): 342.

98 "mysterious, marvellous Indians": D. H. Lawrence, *The Woman Who Rode Away* in The *Woman Who Rode Away and Other Stories* 42.

98 "like bells": *The Woman Who Rode Away* 62.

98 "badly hurt": *DHL Letters* v 144, 5 Oct. 1924, to Clarence Thompson.

98 "steady suppressed growl": *DHL Letters* v 126, 14 Sept. 1924, to Mabel Dodge Luhan.

99 "call them to you": *Lawrence and Brett*, 100.

99 "see the gods again": *DHL Letters* v 77, 23 July 1924, to E. M. Forster.

99 "become part of me": *DHL Letters* v 135, 29 [Sept.] 1924, FL to Anna von Richthofen; my translation.

99 "sometimes I do what he wants": unpublished letter, 14 Oct. 1924, FL to Anna von Richthofen, *sütterlin* 69.

99 "Lawrence looks so good": FL to Anna von Richthofen, 29 [Sept.] 1924, *DHL Letters* v 135.

99 "has been [. . .] excellent": unpublished letter, FL to Anna von Richthofen, 8 Aug. 1924, *sütterlin* 67.

100 "furious": *Lawrence and Brett* 140.

100 "cosmic beasts": D. H. Lawrence, *Mornings in Mexico,* in *Mornings in Mexico and Etruscan Places* (1927; reprinted London: Heinemann, 1956): 65.

100 "affirmed in the Indians": unpublished letter, FL to Mabel Dodge Luhan, 3 July 1930, Yale University.

100 "to interfere [. . .] much space": unpublished letter, FL to Anna von Richthofen, 14 Oct. 1924, *sütterlin* 69.

Chapter 15, "Frightened"

102 "you see the people": *Lawrence and Brett* 160.

102 the Zapotec's cooperative stability: On the Zapotec crisis, even worse after 1912, see Patrick J. McNamara, *Sons of the Sierra: Juárez, Díaz, and the People of Ixtlán, Oaxaca, 1855-1920*

(Chapel Hill: University of North Carolina Press, 2007): 188-205.

102 "these dying, apathetic Indians": unpublished letter, FL to Anna von Richthofen, [19 Feb. 1925], *sütterlin* 71.

103 "just right": *DHL Letters* v 166, 15 Nov. 1924, to Emily King.

103 "never crumbled in an earthquake!": Interview, Michael Squires with José Alvarez Padilla, 19 May 1995, Oaxaca, Mexico.

104 "wasn't well down here": *DHL Letters* v 211, 7 Feb. 1925, to William Hawk.

104 "go your own way": *DHL Letters* v 192, [9 Jan. 1925], to Dorothy Brett.

104 "soft repose [. . .] mystery": D. H. Lawrence, *The Plumed Serpent*, ed. L. D. Clark (Cambridge: Cambridge University Press, 1987): 81.

104 "and to save her": *Ibid.* 103.

105 "just a woman": *Ibid.* 325.

105 "from the volcanic deeps": *Ibid.* 422.

105 "spiritual intimacy whatever": *Ibid.* 423.

105 "a great novel": *DHL Letters* viii 92, [5 March 1925], FL to Friedrich Jaffe.

105 "exhausted [. . .] enormous cactus": unpublished letter, FL to Anna von Richthofen, 21 Jan. 1925, *sütterlin* 70.

105 "have pulled him through": FL to Friedrich Jaffe, [?15 March 1925], *DHL Letters* viii 92; my translation.

105 "bewitched by his Mexico": unpublished letter, FL to Anna von Richthofen, [19 Feb. 1925], *sütterlin* 71.

106 "Mr Lawrence [. . .] immigration officials": *Not I, But the Wind* 151.

106 "The only gods are men": *The Plumed Serpent*, Textual Apparatus 427: line 9 (typescript reading).

107 "to feel better again": FL to Kathryn Herbig, 26 April 1938; quoted in *D. H. Lawrence's Manuscripts* 173-74.

Chapter 16, "The Road to Spotorno"

108 "to get a fresh start": *DHL Letters* v 172, 17 Nov. 1924, to Clarence Thompson.

108 "half awake": *DHL Letters* v 233, 6 April 1925, to Ida Rauh.

108 "himself out to them": unpublished letter, FL to Anna von Richthofen, [c. 22 April 1925], *sütterlin* 73.

109 "hit her on the nose": *Lawrence and Brett* 228.

109 "stronger than mine": FL to Dorothy Brett, 20 Feb. [1925], in "D. H. Lawrence and Frieda Lawrence: Letters to Dorothy Brett," ed. Peter L. Irvine and Anne Kiley, *D. H. Lawrence Review* 9 (1976): 41. Hereafter, "Letters to Dorothy Brett."

109 Scott Murray, who charged them $50: unpublished ledger; checks from D. H. Lawrence to Scott Murray, numbered 65, 69, 75, and 76, totaling $49.75 (Chávez).

109 "never felt less literary": *DHL Letters* v 263, 10 June 1925, to George Conway.

110 "a new gleam, never yet beheld": D. H. Lawrence, "Reflections on the Death of a Porcupine," in *Reflections on the Death of a Porcupine and Other Essays*, ed. Michael Herbert (Cambridge: Cambridge University Press, 1988): 361.

111 "unending materialism": *DHL Letters* v 294, 31 Aug. 1925, to Kyle Crichton.

111 "the hidden stuff": *DHL Letters* v 308, [28 Sept. 1925], to Kyle Crichton.

111 "There *must* be more money!": D. H. Lawrence, "The Rocking Horse Winner," in *The Woman Who Rode Away and Other Stories*, ed. Dieter Mehl and Christa Jansohn (Cambridge: Cambridge University Press, 1995): 230.

112 "a crash to the ground": "The Rocking Horse Winner" 235.

112 "incessant feeling of hostility": *Lawrence and Brett* 252.

112 "balance of $1,002 [. . .] $2,254": unpublished ledger of D. H. Lawrence, checks numbered 84 (21 Sept. 1925) and 88 (21 March 1926), Chase National Bank of the City of New York (Chávez).

113 "And I between": FL to Dorothy Brett, [4 Nov. 1925], "Letters to Dorothy Brett" 55.

113 "girlish, hysterical voice": quoted in *A Composite Biography* iii 10.

113 "pinched and small": Carswell, *The Savage Pilgrimage* 227.

113 "I feel happy – for no reason": FL to Dorothy Brett, [Nov. 1925], "Letters to Dorothy Brett" 57.

Chapter 17, "Compassion and Rage"

114 "coughed like the devil": *DHL Letters* v 332, 4 Nov. 1925, to Dorothy Brett.

114 "Octavian Augustus": *DHL Letters* v 342, 23 Nov. 1925, to Blanche Knopf.

114 "figs and nuts and pears": unpublished letter, FL to Emily King, [26 Nov. 1925], University of Nottingham.

115 "we drew and sang": unpublished letter, FL to Anna von Richthofen, [23 Dec. 1925], *sütterlin* 75.

116 "Look at her false face": *Not I, But the Wind* 179.

116 "worse," he told Brett: *DHL Letters* v 390, [11 Feb. 1926], to Dorothy Brett.

116 "have a nice time": *DHL Letters* v 401, 2 March 1926, to Ada Clarke.

116 "really shattered": quoted in *A Composite Biography* iii 22.

116 "Vengo a Capri": *DHL Letters* v 400, 26 Feb. 1926, to Dorothy Brett.

117 "tired to death": *Lawrence and Brett* 271.

117 "not true to others": *Ibid.* 278.

117 "go away for a time": *Ibid.* 272.

118 "I felt desperate [. . .] It was hopeless": quoted in *Living at the Edge* 316–7 and, with revisions, in Hignett, *Brett* 191–2.

118 "no matter what's happened": *DHL Letters* v 408, [21 March 1926], to Dorothy Brett.

118 "a good many matters": *DHL Letters* v 421, [22 April 1926], to Earl Brewster.

119 "lay the law down": *DHL Letters* v 403, [11 March 1926], to Ada Clarke.

119 "lovely in its way": *DHL Letters* v 447, 3 May 1926, to Margaret King.

119 "I wanted that villa": *Not I, But the Wind* 186.

119 "si estendeva per molte miglia": Interview, Alessandro Mirenda with the author, 9 June 2001.

Chapter 18, "Exposing Their Secret"

121 "I understand by life": unpublished letter, FL to Anna von Richthofen, [28 April 1928], *sütterlin* 79.

122 "in my native Midlands": *DHL Letters* v 521, 2 Sept. 1926, to S. S. Koteliansky.

122 "like summer": *DHL Letters* v 550, 5 Oct. 1926, to Gertrude Cooper.

123 "about the strike": *DHL Letters* v 565, 28 Oct. 1926, to Ada Clarke.

123 "to let off steam": John Turner, ed., "D. H. Lawrence in the Wilkinson Diaries," *D. H. Lawrence Review*, 30 (2002): 27–28; punctuation and paragraphing have been corrected. Hereafter, *Wilkinson Diaries* and date of diary entry.

123 "change the subject": *Wilkinson Diaries* 29, 1 Nov. 1926.

124 "She loved [. . .] have to!": D. H. Lawrence, *The First Lady Chatterley* (London: Heinemann, 1972): 3–5.

125 "he was away": D. H. Lawrence, *John Thomas and Lady Jane* (London: Heinemann, 1972): 7.

125 "of great bells": *The First Lady Chatterley* 35.

125 "Passion has dignity": *DHL Letters* viii 111, [c. 1928], to Barbara Weekley.

126 "played the accompaniments": *Wilkinson Diaries* 35, 30 Jan. 1927.

127 "bottomless pools" of his imagination: *DHL Letters* v 605, 19 Dec. 1926, to Dorothy Brett.

127 "medium build [. . .] military erectness": *John Thomas and Lady Jane* 27.

127 "Our society is insane": *Ibid*. 100.

127 "she had touched God": *Ibid*. 263.

128 "not bad, but beastly": *DHL Letters* v 654, 11 March 1927, to Nancy Pearn.

128 call it "malaria": *Wilkinson Diaries* 43, 10 May 1927.

Chapter 19, "The Final Version"

129 "through the universe": D. H. Lawrence, *Sketches of Etruscan Places*, ed. Simonetta de Filippis (Cambridge: Cambridge University Press, 1992): 60.

130 "keeps coming back": *DHL Letters* viii 105, [22 July 1927], to Caroline Ashby.

130 "hardly knows him": *Wilkinson Diaries* 48, 18 July 1927.

130 "as soon as possible": *DHL Letters* vi 183, 10 Oct. 1927, to Max Mohr.

130 would be called "pornographic": *DHL Letters* vi 182, 10 Oct. 1927, to Alfred Knopf.

130 "no life [. . .] dreadfully sharp": *Wilkinson Diaries* 52, 19–20 Oct. 1927.

131 "as a man, could you?": D. H. Lawrence, *Lady Chatterley's Lover*, ed. Michael Squires (Cambridge: Cambridge University Press, 1993): 53.

132 "quite the gentleman": *Lady Chatterley's Lover* 145.

132 "class of society": Earl and Achsah Brewster, *D. H. Lawrence: Reminiscences and Correspondence* (London: Secker, 1934): 276.

132 "deeper and deeper": *Lady Chatterley's Lover* 134.

132 "have his way [. . .] was dying": *Lady Chatterley's Lover* 246–47.

133 "Dublin mongrel": *Lady Chatterley's Lover* 22.

133 "like an idiot": *Lady Chatterley's Lover* 110.

133 "selfish little horrors: *Lady Chatterley's Lover* 239.

133 "a flame into being": *Lady Chatterley's Lover* 301.

134 "far before" love: *DHL Letters* iv 367, 4 Jan. 1923, to Thomas Seltzer.

134 cheque for $4,000 to Bonbright & Co.: D. H. Lawrence, cheque no. 96, 8 Sept. 1927, Chase National Bank (Chávez).

134 "very weak": unpublished letter, FL to Anna von Richthofen, 28 Dec. 1927, *sütterlin* 77.

134 "determined to [publish] it": *DHL Letters* vi 289, 6 Feb. 1928, to Giuseppe Orioli.

135 "Not a penny!": *Wilkinson Diaries* 61, 15 March 1928.

135 "myself slowly freer": unpublished letter, FL to Anna von Richthofen, [28 April 1928], *sütterlin* 79.

135 "damn and damn them": *DHL Letters* vi 532, 30 Aug. 1928, to Giuseppe Orioli.

Chapter 20, "Where to Go?"

136 "blissfully happy": FL to Witter Bynner, [9 April 1928], in *The Memoirs and Correspondence* 229.

136 "I am already": *DHL Letters* vi 332, 17 March 1928, to Rolf Gardiner.

136 "The novel's price was £2 or $10 for a signed and numbered copy": In March 2008 seven copies of the original Florence Edition were listed for sale at prices ranging from $7,500 to $25,000.

137 "thousands of mistakes": quoted in *Lady Chatterley's Lover* xxviii n16.

137 "fun doing it": *DHL Letters* vi 347, 31 March 1928, to S. S. Koteliansky.

137 "make a cure": *DHL Letters* vi 323, 15 March 1928, to S. S. Koteliansky.

>─◆>─0─◆─◆

137 "he was very ill": Achsah Brewster in Brewsters, *D. H. Lawrence* 281.

138 "I think you [. . .] talk": *DHL Letters* vi 448, [5 July 1928], to Giuseppe Orioli.

138 "without any trouble": Giuseppe Orioli to Harold Mason, 17 Aug. 1928, in *DHL Letters* vi 419 n3.

138 "Damn them all": *DHL Letters* vi 481, 30 July 1928, to S. S. Koteliansky.

138 "no more to America": *DHL Letters* viii 115, 1 Sept. 1928, to Jacob Baker.

138 "magnificent beyond praise": cited in Michael Squires, *The Creation of "Lady Chatterley's Lover"* (Baltimore: Johns Hopkins University Press, 1983): 190.

138 "tormenting cough": *DHL Letters* vi 457, [11 July 1928], to Ada Clarke.

139 "lady die," and so terrify Achsah: Brigit Patmore, cited in *A Composite Biography* iii 259.

139 "dreadful hollow cough": Richard Aldington, cited in *A Composite Biography* iii 253.

139 "I should like [. . .] cold": *DHL Letters* vi 604, 31 Oct. 1928, to S. S. Koteliansky.

139 "foulest book in English literature": cited in *A Composite Biography* iii 263.

140 "Italy this winter": *DHL Letters* vi 502, 12 Aug. 1928, to Bonamy Dobrée.

140 "profits from *Lady Chatterley's Lover* at £1,240": For details see Squires, *Creation of "Lady Chatterley's Lover"* 221–23.

140 "our instincts and our intuitions": D. H. Lawrence, "Insouciance," in *Phoenix II: Uncollected, Unpublished, and Other Prose Works by D. H. Lawrence*, ed. Warren Roberts and Harry T. Moore (New York: Viking, 1959): 534.

140 "in the neck and passes on": D. H. Lawrence, "What does she want?" in D. H. Lawrence, *The Complete Poems*, ed. Vivian de Sola Pinto and F. Warren Roberts (New York: Viking, 1971): 539.

141 "fearlessness": *DHL Letters* vii 78, [20 Dec. 1928], to P. R. Stephensen.

142 "my intuitional consciousness": quoted in Keith Sagar, *D. H. Lawrence's Paintings* (London: Chaucer Press, 2003): 121.

142 "rarely preferred to be alone": Brewster Ghiselin, cited in *A Composite Biography* iii 293.

142 "dirtiest to come—[the price was] 5000 frs!!": *DHL Letters* vii 57, [11 Dec. 1928], to Maria Huxley.

142 "must really try": *DHL Letters* vii 67, [16 Dec. 1928], to Laurence Pollinger.

Chapter 21, "Masses of Mimosa"

143 "What a game life is!": *DHL Letters* viii 111, 20 Dec. 1928, to the Wilkinsons.

143 "to keep [true to] what I am": *DHL Letters* vii 179, 15 Feb. 1929, to P. R. Stephensen.

144 a "healthy" book: D. H. Lawrence, *A Propos of "Lady Chatterley's Lover,"* in *Lady Chatterley's Lover*, ed. Michael Squires (Cambridge: Cambridge University Press, 1993): 307.

144 Titus had [. . .] more than 40,000 francs: D. H. Lawrence, unpublished memorandum, n.d. (Chávez).

144 "my real will to live": *DHL Letters* vii 235, 3 April 1929, to Ottoline Morrell.

144 "two minds about it": *DHL Letters* vii 88, 23 Dec. 1928, to Charles Lahr.

144 "trim the book" into a different shape: *DHL Letters* vii 144, 18 Jan. 1929, to Charles Lahr.

144 "try once more": *DHL Letters* vii 368, 13 July 1929, to Laurence Pollinger.

144 "débâcle [. . .] to expurgate": *DHL Letters* vii 392 n1; original TS at the Copley Library.

144 the secret Third Edition: For details see Craig Munro, "*Lady Chatterley* in London: The Secret Third Edition," in *D. H. Lawrence's "Lady": A New Look at "Lady Chatterley's Lover,"* ed. Michael Squires and Dennis Jackson (Athens: University of Georgia Press, 1985): 222–35.

145 "afraid of the police": *DHL Letters* vii 214, [9 March 1929], to Earl and Achsah Brewster.

145 "don't want my pictures burnt": *DHL Letters* vii 369, 14 July 1929, to Dorothy Warren.

145 "He is so, so frail!": FL to Dorothy Warren , 23 July 1929, in *A Composite Biography* iii 377.

145 "sits and does nothing": Sybille Bedford, *Aldous Huxley: A*

Biography (1974; reprinted New York: Carroll & Graf, 1985): 215.

146 "I try to be cheerful": unpublished letter, FL to Emily King, [Dec. 1929], University of Nottingham.

146 "Why, oh why [. . .] we help it?": *Not I, But the Wind* 288.

146 Dr. Andrew Morland . . . French sanatorium at Vence to get well: Dr. Morland believed that Lawrence had suffered from tuberculosis "for a very long time—probably 10 or 15 years" (quoted in *A Composite Biography* iii 424).

146 "I am [. . .] very short time": unpublished letter, S. S. Koteliansky to DHL, 5 Feb. [1930], Chávez; quoted by permission of Catherine Stoye.

146 "*very* frail [. . .] to the good": FL to Dorothy Brett, [Nov. 1929], "Letters to Dorothy Brett" 98.

147 "nothing for me": *DHL Letters* vii 645, [12 Feb. 1930], to Maria Huxley.

147 "in the living night": D. H. Lawrence, "Ship of Death," *The Complete Poems* 964.

148 "His death [. . .] simple greatness": unpublished letter, FL to Nancy Pearn, 6 March 1930, University of Nottingham; partially published in *DHL Letters* vii 15.

148 "his love for life": FL to E. M. Forster, [20 March 1930], in *Selected Letters of E. M. Forster*, ed. Mary Lago and P. N. Furbank (Cambridge: Harvard University Press, 1985): 91 n1.

Chapter 22, "Without a Will"

149 "the realest thing to me": unpublished letter, FL to S. S. Koteliansky, [16 April 1930], British Library.

149 "*all* the interest is mine": FL to Edward Titus, [25 April 1930]; quoted in *Frieda Lawrence and Her Circle*, ed. Harry T. Moore and Dale B. Montague (Basingstoke: Macmillan, 1981; Hamden, CT: Archon Books, 1981): 8.

149 "stupid" and "unpractical": Robert Nichols, as quoted in Bedford, *Aldous Huxley: A Biography* 226.

149 "by my instinct": unpublished letter, FL to Laurence Pollinger, 21 Jan. 1931, HRHRC.

150 "clearer for me": FL to Witter Bynner, 23 July 1930, *The Memoirs and Correspondence* 239.

150 "as if [. . .] splendid show": unpublished letter, FL to Ottoline Morrell, [12 May 1931], HRHRC.

150 Barbara [. . .] to England to recuperate: Frieda hinted, and Mabel Dodge Luhan later confirmed, that Barbara Weekley had contracted syphilis.

151 "cruel to me this year": FL to Edward Titus, 5 Dec. 1930; quoted in *Frieda Lawrence and Her Circle* 24.

151 "Frieda was [. . .] Lawrence estate": Interview, Stefano Ravagli with Stefania Michelucci, Spotorno, Italy, 5 Sept. 1998; quoted in *Living at the Edge* 373.

152 "have [recently] killed themselves": unpublished letter, Maria Cristina Chambers to Giuseppe Orioli, 13 March 1931; quoted by permission of Rosalind Wells.

152 "more truly [Lawrence's] widow than Frieda": unpublished letter, Dorothy Brett to Alfred Stieglitz, [2 June 1931], Yale University; quoted in *Living at the Edge* 369.

152 "that life of otherness": unpublished letter, FL to Mabel Dodge Luhan, [6 Aug. 1932], Yale University; quoted in *Living at the Edge* 371.

152 "Angelino [. . .] We all like him": unpublished letter, Mabel Dodge Luhan to Una Jeffers, 3 June 1931, University of California at Berkeley; quoted in *Living at the Edge* 371.

153 "I do like [. . .] gentleness and warmth": unpublished letter, FL to Dorothy Brett, [10 Feb. 1932], Yale University.

153 "being without money": unpublished letter, FL to Philip Morrell, 19 Feb. 1931, HRHRC.

154 "money to go to George": unpublished letter (copy), FL to Ada Clarke, [25 June 1930], British Library.

154 "hatred of Frieda": Emile Delavenay, "Sandals and Scholarship," *D. H. Lawrence Review* 9 (1976): 410.

154 "your brother [. . .] the wife": unpublished letter, FL to Emily King, [1 Nov. 1930]; quoted in Christie's sale catalog, 16 Oct. 1985.

Chapter 23, "Manuscripts and Money"

155 "our life together": unpublished letter, FL to Laurence Pollinger, [7 Nov. 1932], HRHRC.

155 "anger crawling about": letter, Aldous Huxley to Naomi Mitchison, quoted in Bedford, *Aldous Huxley: A Biography* 274.

155 "I'm so busy [. . .] to bursting – ": unpublished letter, FL to Knud Merrild, 20 Dec. 1932, HRHRC.

156 "means everything to me – ": unpublished letter, FL to Mabel Dodge Luhan, 2 Feb. 1934, Yale University.

157 "like my life with Lawrence was": unpublished letter, FL to Laurence Pollinger, [25 June 1934], HRHRC.

157 "I have [. . .] work and sunshine": FL to Martha Gordon Crotch, [Aug. 1934], quoted in Crotch, *Memories of Frieda Lawrence* (Edinburgh: Travara Press, 1975): 26.

158 "with all the scandal": unpublished letter, FL to Laurence Pollinger, 22 April 1935, HRHRC.

158 "so shocked and angry": FL to Mabel Dodge Luhan (unsent), [Aug. 1935]; quoted in *Memoirs and Correspondence* 251.

158 "simply overwhelming": Jake Zeitlin to FL, 20 Oct. 1936, quoted in *D. H. Lawrence's Manuscripts* 58.

159 "I liked her [. . .] a satyr": quoted in *Living at the Edge* 380–81.

160 "being in another world": Craig Smith, *Sing My Whole Life Song: Jenny Vincent's Life in Folk Music and Activism* (Albuquerque: University of New Mexico Press, 2007): 21.

160 "without being possessive": Interview, Jenny Wells Vincent with the author, 16 July 1989; quoted in *D. H. Lawrence's Manuscripts* 7.

160 "rather limited resources": letter of 27 April 1937; quoted in *D. H. Lawrence's Manuscripts* 87.

Chapter 24, "A Home on the Coast"

162 "to sell to Harvard –": FL to Jake Zeitlin, Sept. 1937, quoted in *D. H. Lawrence's Manuscripts* 112.

163 "Frieda is continually [. . .] Aldous is working": letter, Maria Huxley to Eddy Sackville-West, 23 June 1937; quoted in Bedford, *Aldous Huxley: A Biography* 347.

164 "most God-awful bore": quoted in *D. H. Lawrence's Manuscripts* 16.

165 "like the women [. . .] a great deal": Grace Hubble, unpublished journal, 12 May 1938, Huntington Library; quoted in *Living at the Edge* 390.

165 "the best in America": unpublished letter, FL to Dudley Nichols, 25 Aug. 1944, Yale University.

165 "already an old [. . .] hopelessly undramatic": quoted in *Living at the Edge* 396.

166 "I always loved it best": unpublished letter, FL to Dudley Nichols, 2 March 1944, Yale University.

166 "makes me so angry": FL to Richard Aldington, 8 April 1941; quoted in *Frieda Lawrence and Her Circle* 80.

167 "the best in oneself": unpublished letter, FL to Dudley Nichols, 26 July 1945, Yale University.

167 "being fun here": unpublished letter, FL to Brett, 14 Feb. 1947, University of New Mexico.

Chapter 25, "A Pair in Perspective"

169 "little Mexican beanie": Telephone interview, Miranda Masocco (Levy) with the author, 7 May 1999; quoted in *Living at the Edge* 413.

170 "felt free to be myself": unpublished letter, FL to Richard Aldington, [c. 30 April 1950], Southern Illinois University.

171 "totalled 3,226,556 copies": See Gerald J. Pollinger, "*Lady Chatterley's Lover:* A View from Lawrence's Literary Executor," in *D. H. Lawrence's "Lady": A New Look at "Lady Chatterley's Lover,"* ed. Michael Squires and Dennis Jackson (Athens: University of Georgia Press, 1985): 238.

171 "liked their adulation": Telephone interview, Amalia de Schulthess with the author, 9 July 1989; quoted in *D. H. Lawrence's Manuscripts* 22.

172 "live so very much longer": FL to Warren and Pat Roberts, 1 Jan. 1955; quoted in *D. H. Lawrence's Manuscripts* 214.

172 "than he ever meant to": FL to Warren Roberts, 30 Nov. 1954; quoted in *D. H. Lawrence's Manuscripts* 212.

172 "legally bind [. . .] call the deal off": unpublished draft letter, Angelo Ravagli to Harry Ransom, 24 Nov. 1954; quoted by permission of Barbara Horgan.

172 "so quaint [. . .] flashing fire": Louis Gibbons, "The D. H. Lawrences," 139, 142; unpublished memoir (1960) in the possession of the author.

173 "her rare gift of life": quoted in *El Crepusculo*, 16 Aug. 1956.

174 "height of all human experience": FL to Edward Gilbert, 17 Sept. 1944; quoted in *Memoirs & Correspondence* 295.

Index

INDEX